# SMARTPHONE APP THAT PRODUCES ENERGY ON THE PHONE SCREEN, ENERGY PRODUCTION DIGITAL SOLAR PANEL

The Revolutionary Application to Produce Sustainable Energy without a solar panel on your roof

by:
## DANILO TADEU VIEIRA DE SOUSA

# DEDICATION

The world is facing an unsustainable climate problem, caused by economically industrialized countries. Greed for unsustainable economic growth accelerates global pollution, increasing global warming. I dedicate this book and my Clean and Fast Energy Production Application project to all polluting countries that still resist implementing sustainable and global systems. I also dedicate this work to powerful lobbyists who do not invest in truly sustainable projects, which can end pollution in just two years, and to all those who neglect to invest in sustainable and innovative environmental solutions. May this book serve as a call to action for a cleaner, more sustainable future for all.

Copyright © 2024 - DANILO TADEU VIEIRA DE SOUSA

All rights reserved

# PRESENTATION

This book explores a revolutionary technology to produce digital energy directly on your smartphone, without the need for solar panels on the roof of your home. The innovation presented promises to significantly help reduce global warming and will teach all people how to generate digital energy, simply by downloading the application that produces energy. Once installed on the phone, the app allows for instant energy production and integration with the local operator, enabling financial gains in domestic or industrial production. The reader will have the opportunity to get to know the monograph of my postgraduate degree in Environmental Engineering, in addition to the patent certificate from the INPI (National Institute of Industrial Property). This book is a complete guide to learning how to produce digital energy without the need for solar panels on the roof, ideal for those who live in apartments. With 75% of the world's population living in apartments, this technology will facilitate energy production in an efficient and sustainable way. Follow this journey of digital innovation and learn how to produce the energy of the future with this inspiring read.

# SUMÁRIO

1 INTRODUÇÃO ........................................................................ 1

2 METHODOLOGY ................................................................... 5

3 GLOBAL ENERGY TRANSITION: A NEW PARADIGM .... 7
   3.1   THE IMPACT OF FOSSIL FUEL DEPENDENCE ON GLOBAL WARMING ................................................................. 7
   3.2   GLOBAL CHALLENGES OF ENERGY SECURITY AND SUSTAINABILITY ....................................................................... 9
   3.3   INTERNATIONAL AGREEMENTS AND PUBLIC POLICIES PROMOTING RENEWABLE ENERGY ........ 12
   3.4   THE ROLE OF A LOW-CARBON ECONOMY IN THE REDEFINITION OF ENERGY MATRICES ..................... 14
   3.5   FUTURE PERSPECTIVES FOR THE ENERGY TRANSITION: TRENDS AND FORECASTS .................... 17

4 PHOTOVOLTAIC SOLAR ENERGY: A PILLAR OF THE ENERGY TRANSITION ........................................................ 21
   4.1   FUNDAMENTALS OF PHOTOVOLTAIC SOLAR ENERGY: PRINCIPLES AND OPERATION .................... 22
   4.2   THE GLOBAL EXPANSION OF PHOTOVOLTAIC ENERGY: DATA AND GROWTH WORLDWIDE .......... 24
   4.3   TECHNOLOGICAL INNOVATIONS IN PHOTOVOLTAIC CELLS: NEW GENERATIONS AND MATERIALS ................................................................................ 26
   4.4   INTEGRATION OF SOLAR ENERGY INTO POWER GRIDS: CHALLENGES AND OPPORTUNITIES ............ 28
   4.5   ECONOMIC ASPECTS: COST-BENEFIT AND INCENTIVES FOR SOLAR ENERGY ADOPTION ........ 30

5 INNOVATIONS AND TECHNOLOGICAL SOLUTIONS IN DISTRIBUTED ENERGY GENERATION .................... 33
   5.1   DISTRIBUTED ENERGY GENERATION: CONCEPT AND GLOBAL OVERVIEW ............................................... 34
   5.2   INNOVATIVE CASES: NEW PRODUCTS AND BUSINESS MODELS IN THE SOLAR ENERGY SECTOR ....................................................................................... 36

5.3 MOBILE ENERGY: TECHNOLOGICAL INNOVATIONS IN DISTRIBUTED AND VIRTUAL SOLAR ENERGY GENERATION ..................................... 38
    5.3.1 Remote and Virtual Solar Energy Generation: Optimizing Access to Renewable Energy ........... 38
    5.3.2 Real-Time Monitoring Systems and Energy Production Monetization ..................................... 41
    5.3.3 Opportunities for Energy and Financial Inclusion Through Digital Platforms .................................. 44

**6 CONCLUSION** .................................................................... 47

**REFERÊNCIAS** ..................................................................... 51

**PATENT CERTIFICATE IN ENGLISH** .................................... 61

**PATENT CERTIFICATE IN PORTUGUESE** ........................... 83

**SOBRE O AUTOR** ............................................................... 89

# 1 INTRODUÇÃO

The global energy transition has become a central theme in discussions on sustainability due to the urgent need to reduce reliance on fossil fuels and mitigate the impacts of climate change. Within this context, photovoltaic solar energy stands out as one of the most promising renewable technologies, playing a critical role thanks to its ability to generate clean electricity and its potential for decentralization, particularly through distributed generation.

Nevertheless, despite significant advancements in the photovoltaic sector, there are still areas that require further exploration, particularly in regard to technological innovations, the integration of these solutions into electrical grids, and the socioeconomic and environmental impacts of this transition.

This study is justified by the relevance of photovoltaic solar energy in the transition to a more sustainable energy matrix. As global energy demand continues to rise and the pressure for solutions that reduce greenhouse gas emissions intensifies, it is essential to deepen the analysis of how photovoltaic energy can contribute to energy sustainability. The study aims to address existing research gaps by discussing recent technological innovations and opportunities provided by distributed generation, as well as by tackling the challenges involved.

Moreover, by exploring the environmental and socioeconomic impacts of these technologies, the study offers a significant contribution to the field, highlighting the crucial role of distributed generation in strengthening local economies.

In this context, the study seeks to answer the following central question: how can photovoltaic solar energy drive the global energy transition, considering technological, economic, and environmental challenges, and what is the role of distributed generation in this process?

The objectives of this study were designed to address this key question. The general objective is to highlight the role of photovoltaic energy in the global energy transition, with an emphasis on technological innovations and the development of distributed generation, while also discussing the environmental and socioeconomic impacts within the context of sustainability. The specific objectives include identifying the main challenges and trends in the global energy transition, emphasizing the impact of dependence on fossil fuels and the future prospects for energy sustainability; explaining the fundamentals of photovoltaic solar energy and analyzing recent technological innovations, addressing the challenges and opportunities for its integration into electrical grids; and describing technological innovations applied to distributed generation, focusing on innovation case studies, emerging business models, and the energy and financial inclusion enabled by digital platforms.

The structure of this article has been organized into five chapters. The first chapter presents an introduction to the topic and the research problem. The second chapter discusses the new paradigm of the global energy transition, addressing the impact of dependence on fossil fuels, the challenges of energy security and sustainability, and public policies aimed at promoting renewable energy sources. The third chapter focuses on photovoltaic solar energy as a cornerstone of the energy transition, outlining its fundamentals, the global growth of this technology, and the innovations driving its development. The fourth chapter analyzes technological innovations in distributed energy generation, highlighting new products, business models, and technological solutions. Finally, the fifth chapter presents the conclusions, summarizing the main contributions of the study to the field.

# 2 METHODOLOGY

This research was characterized as a bibliographic study aimed at analyzing photovoltaic energy within the context of the global energy transition, with an emphasis on technological innovations and the sustainability associated with distributed generation. The choice of this research approach was justified by the extensive range of materials available in academic databases, which enabled a deep exploration of different aspects of the topic and access to relevant studies previously conducted in the field of renewable energy.

The bibliographic method allowed for the construction of a robust theoretical framework regarding emerging technologies applied to photovoltaic solar energy and their role in mitigating environmental and socioeconomic impacts.

The materials used in this research were sourced from widely recognized academic repositories, such as Google Scholar, SciELO (Scientific Electronic Library Online), and the CAPES Thesis and Dissertation Repository, as well as specialized journals in the field of renewable energy. Additionally, international databases such as ScienceDirect and IEEE Xplore were consulted to collect high-impact articles and publications, particularly those focused on technological innovations in solar energy and advancements in distributed generation. The research prioritized sources addressing technological development, public policies, economic aspects, and socio-environmental issues related to photovoltaic energy.

The keywords used to search for materials were selected based on the main topics addressed in the study and included the terms: "photovoltaic energy," "energy transition," "distributed generation," "technological innovations," "sustainability," "renewable energy integration," and "energy public policies." These keywords facilitated the identification of a variety of relevant academic sources, focusing on the challenges and opportunities photovoltaic solar energy offers within the context of the transition to a low-carbon economy.

The materials analyzed included scientific articles, monographs, theses, dissertations, and books published in Portuguese and English. The use of documents in two languages broadened the scope of the research, enabling the inclusion of both international and national contributions on the topic. Moreover, the diversity of sources ensured a multidimensional approach, allowing for an understanding of both the technological development and practical applicability of solar energy innovations, as well as the impact of public policies across different regions. The bibliographic review was essential for identifying research gaps and connecting emerging innovations to the broader context of energy sustainability.

The analysis of the materials was guided by criteria of relevance and timeliness, prioritizing works published in the last ten years, except in cases of foundational theoretical studies necessary for understanding the topic. More recent publications provided an up-to-date perspective on technological trends and public policies shaping the photovoltaic energy landscape, while older studies offered a solid theoretical basis for understanding the development of photovoltaic technologies and distributed generation.

# 3 GLOBAL ENERGY TRANSITION: A NEW PARADIGM

## 3.1 THE IMPACT OF FOSSIL FUEL DEPENDENCE ON GLOBAL WARMING

The world's dependence on fossil fuels and its impact on global warming represent one of the most pressing challenges of the 21st century. The relationship between greenhouse gas emissions—caused by the burning of oil, coal, and natural gas—and rising global temperatures has fueled intense debate about the future of energy. This section examines how fossil fuel dependence exacerbates global warming and the effects this has on the climate, ecosystems, and society. Additionally, it explores why this energy model continues to persist despite the growing number of international policies aimed at mitigating its effects.

According to Annamalai et al. (2018), the burning of fossil fuels is the primary source of carbon dioxide ($CO_2$) emissions, which significantly contribute to the greenhouse effect. Since the onset of the Industrial Revolution, these emissions have risen drastically due to the growing demand for energy to support transportation and industrial production. This pattern of energy development has led to a buildup of $CO_2$ in the atmosphere, where it can persist for centuries, intensifying global warming.

Expanding on this perspective, Isa-Yusuf and Binzaid (2020) emphasize that electricity generation from fossil fuel sources, particularly coal and natural gas, is one of the main sectors driving the increase in emissions, accounting for a significant share of air pollution.

The environmental consequences of this dependence are extensive and alarming. The extraction of fossil fuels, especially through methods such as hydraulic fracturing, causes environmental degradation and releases methane, a greenhouse gas that is even more potent than $CO_2$ (Kari, 2024). In addition to direct emissions from combustion, the extraction and transportation processes for fossil fuels produce large amounts of methane, further exacerbating the negative effects on the climate. Therefore, the continued exploitation of these resources is intrinsically tied to the intensification of climate change.

This reality is further underscored by Huntingford et al. (2023), who note that the ongoing use of fossil fuels also carries significant social and economic implications. For example, the recent conflict between Russia and Ukraine demonstrated how dependence on fossil energy resources can render entire regions vulnerable to supply crises and price volatility.

In Europe, for instance, the shortage of natural gas forced the reactivation of coal-fired power plants, which, in turn, further increased greenhouse gas emissions, creating a vicious cycle of dependence and environmental degradation. As a result, maintaining an energy model reliant on fossil fuels not only harms the environment but also exposes countries to substantial economic and political risks (Huntingford et al., 2023).

On the other hand, Annamalai et al. (2018) point out that despite growing concerns about climate change, the transition to cleaner energy sources still faces numerous obstacles. Even with the targets set by international agreements such as the Paris Agreement, infrastructure and economic systems remain heavily reliant on fossil fuels. According to the authors, transitioning to renewable energy requires substantial investments, and the pace of this transition has been slow, particularly in countries whose economies depend on oil and gas exports. This underscores the complexity and depth of the challenge of reducing global $CO_2$ emissions.

While initiatives to mitigate global warming are widely recognized, the current reality is that dependence on fossil fuels remains a significant barrier. For an effective energy transition to occur, it will require a combination of political will, technological innovation, and a reorganization of global economic structures. As Isa-Yusuf and Binzaid (2020) emphasize, only a drastic reduction in fossil fuel consumption will make it possible to mitigate the negative impacts already being felt on the global climate.

In conclusion, the persistent dependence on fossil fuels represents one of the greatest challenges in combating global warming. This issue is deeply intertwined with economic, political, and environmental interests, necessitating a paradigm shift to avoid the worst projected climate scenarios.

In the next chapter, the topic of "Global Challenges of Energy Security and Sustainability" will be addressed, examining how the world can balance its energy needs with the urgency of promoting more sustainable practices. The importance of this topic lies in the fact that, without such a shift, efforts to curb global warming may prove insufficient.

## 3.2 GLOBAL CHALLENGES OF ENERGY SECURITY AND SUSTAINABILITY

Energy security and sustainability are two of the greatest global challenges of our time, particularly in the context of a transition to a low-carbon economy. The intersection of these issues creates a complex scenario in which ensuring a reliable energy supply while promoting environmental sustainability represents one of the most pressing dilemmas faced by governments, industries, and society.

This chapter seeks to explore the primary tensions and solutions associated with these challenges, discussing the various aspects of energy security, efficiency, and the transition to renewable energy sources. By doing so, it aims to provide a deeper understanding of how these issues are critical to the future of global energy policies and their direct impact on the sustainable development of nations.

According to Gutierrez (2021), energy security involves not only ensuring a reliable supply of energy but also diversifying energy sources and promoting efficiency within energy systems. In OECD countries, for example, the balance between energy security, sustainability, and efficiency has been at the core of their energy policies.

Although liberalizing reforms have reduced the direct role of the state as an owner in the energy sector, its role as a regulator and coordinator has intensified, particularly in the pursuit of solutions that enable the transition to a low-carbon economy (Gutierrez, 2021). This indicates that ensuring long-term energy security requires the state to play an active role in fostering resilient and sustainable energy infrastructure.

Kocaslan (2022) adds to this analysis by discussing the importance of energy efficiency in the context of energy security and sustainability. The author asserts that energy efficiency is regarded as one of the key strategies for reducing the demand for new energy sources while simultaneously minimizing environmental impacts. However, as Kocaslan highlights, improving energy efficiency is no simple task, as it involves a variety of factors, including technological innovations, changes in public policies, and the need to adapt societal consumption habits. By prioritizing energy efficiency, countries can not only reduce their energy costs but also mitigate risks associated with reliance on external energy sources.

Elkhatat and Al-Muhtaseb (2024) stress that addressing climate change and ensuring energy security requires a coordinated approach that integrates both energy and environmental policies. Global warming has heightened the urgency for more sustainable energy sources, placing even greater pressure on governments to promote the transition to renewables.

This transition is essential not only for reducing greenhouse gas emissions but also for enabling countries to tackle global energy challenges without compromising the environment (Elkhatat; Al-Muhtaseb, 2024). This underscores the necessity of aligning energy and environmental policies to achieve a sustainable future.

On the other hand, the transition to renewable energy also creates new vulnerabilities, as Rato (2022) points out by explaining that reliance on certain critical minerals essential for green energy technologies, such as cobalt and lithium, may lead to new geopolitical imbalances. Countries that dominate the production of these resources, such as China and the Democratic Republic of Congo, could emerge as key players in the global energy landscape, raising fresh concerns regarding supply security. This context highlights the complexity of the energy transition, where new challenges arise as old issues are mitigated.

Zaytsev et al. (2023) reinforces this perspective by discussing the impact of energy security on regional sustainable development strategies, emphasizing that dependence on external energy sources can limit sustainable economic growth and expose regions to significant vulnerabilities, especially during times of crisis.

Thus, increasing energy autonomy by diversifying the energy mix and promoting the use of local energy sources becomes a priority to ensure both economic and environmental sustainability. This regional approach underscores the idea that solutions for energy security and sustainability are not solely global but also local, requiring strategic coordination across various levels of government (Zaytsev et al., 2023).

Ensuring global energy security and promoting environmental sustainability are therefore interconnected and challenging tasks. The transition to a cleaner energy matrix demands that governments and industries work together, developing innovative policies and collaborating internationally to mitigate the effects of climate change and reduce reliance on non-renewable energy sources.

In the next chapter, international agreements and public policies promoting renewable energy will be discussed, focusing on how global agreements can play a crucial role in facilitating this energy transition and fostering multilateral collaborations to address shared challenges.

## 3.3 INTERNATIONAL AGREEMENTS AND PUBLIC POLICIES PROMOTING RENEWABLE ENERGY

International agreements and public policies promoting renewable energy are essential tools for driving the global energy transition, particularly in the fight against climate change. Over the past several years, numerous nations have made international commitments aimed at fostering a more sustainable energy matrix that is less dependent on fossil fuels.

According to Peyerl et al. (2022), the Paris Agreement is one of the most significant milestones in advancing sustainable energy policies, with clear goals to limit the rise in global temperatures to less than 2°C. In this context, renewable energy sources play a central role in decarbonization strategies, with signatory countries implementing public policies aimed at increasing the share of renewables in their energy mix.

Moreover, the creation of financial mechanisms such as the Green Climate Fund has been crucial in supporting developing nations in the implementation of these policies, enabling a more equitable energy transition.

One of the primary challenges faced by countries in promoting renewable energy, as discussed by Bento et al. (2019), is the need for robust public policies that incentivize investment in new technologies. Countries that have implemented mechanisms such as auctions and feed-in tariffs, like China and Brazil, have experienced significant increases in their installed renewable energy capacity. However, regulatory instability and a lack of consistent incentives remain barriers to the expansion of renewable energy sources in many regions of the world. This underscores the importance of stable and long-term policies.

The adoption of fiscal incentive policies, such as the extrafiscal measures discussed by Mencucini (2022), has also shown promising results in promoting renewable energy. This approach uses green tax norms to encourage the use of clean energy sources, integrating them into the tax system as a way to induce sustainable behavior. In countries like Brazil, where energy crises caused by droughts are recurrent, tax-induced policies have played a fundamental role in ensuring the continuity of the energy transition.

In addition to fiscal and regulatory incentives, technological advancement is another crucial factor for the success of renewable energy incentive policies in Latin America. The implementation of more efficient technologies, such as solar and wind energy, is often driven by public policies that promote innovation and research in the energy sector (Taveira, 2023). However, the author emphasizes that for these technologies to achieve widespread adoption, greater collaboration between the public and private sectors is necessary, as well as the strengthening of regional agreements to encourage the sharing of knowledge and resources.

As noted by Paixão and Miranda (2017), the implementation of these policies varies significantly between countries. While China has achieved remarkable results by adopting a robust industrial policy focused on the production of renewable energy equipment, Brazil, despite having a diversified energy matrix, faces challenges in aligning its renewable energy supply with growing demand. This contrast underscores the importance of public policies tailored to the economic and geographical specificities of each nation, ensuring that the energy transition is not only efficient but also sustainable in the long term.

In conclusion, international agreements and public policies are key components for promoting the use of renewable energy and, consequently, mitigating the impacts of climate change. However, it is essential that these policies are supported by regulatory stability, appropriate fiscal incentives, and technological investments to ensure that their benefits can be fully realized.

## 3.4 THE ROLE OF A LOW-CARBON ECONOMY IN THE REDEFINITION OF ENERGY MATRICES

The transition to a low-carbon economy has emerged as one of the greatest challenges—and simultaneously one of the greatest opportunities—of the 21st century, particularly regarding the redefinition of global energy matrices. It is crucial to examine how this transition is transforming the way countries generate and consume energy and to discuss the role of renewable technologies and public policies driving this shift.

According to Brigido et al. (2023), a low-carbon economy requires the implementation of new energy technologies capable of replacing fossil fuels such as oil and coal with cleaner alternatives like solar, wind, and biofuels. One of the most striking examples of this shift is the growing use of lithium for the production of lithium-ion batteries, which are essential for renewable energy storage and sustainable urban mobility through electric vehicles. This transformation not only reduces $CO_2$ emissions but also creates new value chains in the global economy as the demand for strategic minerals like lithium increases.

As highlighted by Teixeira et al. (2024), the production of biofuels also plays a critical role in the transition to a more sustainable energy matrix. In Brazil, the sugarcane industry has been a pioneer in the production of ethanol, a significant renewable energy source that directly contributes to the decarbonization of the transportation sector.

However, the future energy matrix will likely involve the coexistence of multiple technologies, including vehicle electrification and the use of biofuels, highlighting the need for flexibility in energy policy formulation (Teixeira et al., 2024). This scenario underscores the importance of public policies that encourage innovation and the integration of diverse clean energy sources.

De Blasio and Zheng (2023) emphasize that for a low-carbon economy to be effective, energy value chains must be reconfigured. The transition to renewable energy is not merely about replacing technologies but also about restructuring global energy markets and supply chains. The development of technologies such as renewable hydrogen and large-scale energy storage is critical to ensuring a stable energy supply, even in the face of the intermittency of sources like solar and wind.

As Pflugmann (2020) notes, the shift to a low-carbon economy is also redefining the geopolitics of energy. As countries transition their energy matrices, those that have historically been major exporters of fossil fuels, such as oil, may lose geopolitical influence, while nations with abundant renewable resources, such as wind and solar, are emerging as new global leaders. This realignment has profound implications for global energy security, as economies will need to ensure reliable and sustainable access to these new energy sources.

Additionally, Carvalho et al. (2023) stress that emission mitigation policies must be carefully planned to maximize abatement potential in productive sectors. In Brazil, for example, energy generation—largely based on hydropower—is already relatively clean, but the country continues to face challenges in the transportation sector and in waste management.

To meet the emission reduction targets outlined in the Paris Agreement, it will be essential to implement additional policies to promote renewable energy and energy efficiency (Carvalho; Magalhães; Domingues, 2023). These measures will have a significant impact on reshaping the country's energy matrix.

In conclusion, the transition to a low-carbon economy is transforming global energy matrices, creating new economic opportunities and technological challenges. However, for this transformation to succeed, a coordinated effort among governments, businesses, and civil society is required to implement effective public policies and ensure energy security.

The next chapter will address future perspectives for the energy transition: trends and forecasts, discussing technological trends and projections for the development of new energy sources in the coming years, while highlighting how these advancements will shape the future of economies worldwide.

## 3.5 FUTURE PERSPECTIVES FOR THE ENERGY TRANSITION: TRENDS AND FORECASTS

The trends for the energy transition in the coming decades point to a scenario of profound transformations in global energy matrices. The rapid reduction in the costs of renewable energy technologies, combined with growing political and social pressure for decarbonization, is shaping the future of the sector. It is, therefore, important to analyze these trends, focusing on projections regarding the role of renewable energy, technological innovations, and the challenges that arise in the pursuit of a cleaner and more efficient energy system.

According to Way et al. (2022), the costs of renewable energy technologies, such as photovoltaic solar and wind power, have decreased significantly in recent decades, in stark contrast to the volatility of fossil fuel prices. This downward cost trend has been a key driver for the expansion of renewable energy sources, suggesting that a rapid transition to a green energy system could result in significant economic savings, even without factoring in environmental benefits. This underscores the economic feasibility of the energy transition while highlighting the importance of public policies that incentivize the adoption of these technologies.

Akaev and Davydova (2021) assert that emerging technologies, such as green hydrogen and smart grids, will play a crucial role in reducing global carbon emissions. The use of hydrogen as an alternative energy source is seen as a promising pathway, although challenges related to its storage and cost must still be addressed.

Moreover, the advancement of smart grids will enable greater integration of intermittent renewable sources, such as solar and wind, ensuring greater stability for the energy system. The development of these technologies will be critical for a sustainable transition, providing increased flexibility and efficiency in energy management (Akaev; Davydova, 2021).

On the other hand, Bazilian et al. (2020) emphasize that energy transition scenarios are not uniform across different regions of the world. While European countries are making rapid progress toward decarbonization, other regions, such as South America and Southeast Asia, face additional challenges, including reliance on fossil fuels and technological limitations. The "European Green Deal" serves as an example of how the implementation of rigorous climate policies can drive the transition, but the success of this approach depends on international cooperation and multilateral efforts to overcome economic and geopolitical barriers. This highlights the importance of coordinated global action to ensure that the transition is equitable and efficient.

In addition, Pimentel (2023) explores energy transition scenarios for Brazil through 2040, highlighting the country's contradictory position. With more than 48% of its energy matrix composed of renewable sources, Brazil is still one of the largest oil producers in the world. According to Pimentel, the challenge lies in expanding the share of renewable sources, such as solar and wind energy, while maintaining the export of fossil fuel commodities, which are vital to the national economy. This dilemma is representative of the challenges faced by developing countries in transitioning to a low-carbon economy.

Breyer et al. (2023) note that by 2050, renewable energy sources are expected to account for more than 70% of the energy matrix in many European countries, with solar and wind energy playing a prominent role. Studies indicate that the levelized cost of electricity (LCOE) for these sources will continue to decline, making them increasingly competitive with fossil fuels.

However, Breyer et al. (2023) also warn of the critical need for investments in energy storage technologies, such as batteries, to ensure that this transition occurs efficiently and securely. They underscore the importance of aligning technological innovation with incentive policies to accelerate decarbonization.

In conclusion, forecasts for the energy transition point to a future where renewable sources will dominate the global energy matrix, driven by cost reductions, technological innovation, and political pressures for decarbonization. However, regional challenges and the need for international cooperation remain significant obstacles.

# 4 PHOTOVOLTAIC SOLAR ENERGY: A PILLAR OF THE ENERGY TRANSITION

Photovoltaic solar energy plays a central role in the global energy transition, serving as one of the most promising solutions for reducing dependence on fossil fuels. Over the following sections, the fundamental principles underlying this technology, its impact on energy generation, and its influence on global markets will be explored. Additionally, recent innovations that are enhancing the efficiency of photovoltaic systems and the future prospects for the expansion of this energy source will be discussed. The goal is to provide a comprehensive understanding of how solar cells function, their growth trajectory, and the opportunities presented by technological advancements.

The growth of solar energy worldwide does not come without challenges, particularly regarding its integration into electrical grids and the economic impact of this transformation. Factors such as the cost-effectiveness of photovoltaic systems and governmental incentives will be examined to uncover the elements that facilitate or hinder this transition. By the end of this analysis, readers are expected to understand not only the environmental and economic advantages of solar energy but also the technical and regulatory obstacles that must be overcome to ensure its widespread and effective adoption on a global scale.

## 4.1 FUNDAMENTALS OF PHOTOVOLTAIC SOLAR ENERGY: PRINCIPLES AND OPERATION

Photovoltaic solar energy, which converts sunlight into electricity, is a cornerstone of the energy transition to renewable sources. It is essential to examine the principles and operation of this system, highlighting its key components and the mechanism behind photovoltaic conversion.

The basic principle of photovoltaic solar energy is the direct conversion of solar radiation into electricity through photovoltaic cells. According to Sakthivadivel et al. (2021), this conversion occurs through the photoelectric effect, where the energy from sunlight photons is absorbed by semiconductor materials, typically silicon. This absorption generates free electrons, which create an electric current. This process continues as long as sunlight is present, and the electricity generated can be used immediately or stored in batteries for later use.

Dimitriev et al. (2019) add that the efficiency of solar conversion depends on several factors, including the quality of semiconductor materials, the intensity of solar radiation, and ambient temperature. In regions with higher solar incidence, such as Brazil, conditions are ideal for the installation of high-efficiency photovoltaic systems. However, the challenge remains in improving energy storage capacity, as photovoltaic production is intermittent and varies with the daily and seasonal solar cycles.

The evolution of photovoltaic technologies has been accelerated by research and development into new materials and solar cell configurations. Silicon cells, which are widely used, achieve efficiencies of up to 27%. However, new generations of cells, such as thin-film and perovskite-based cells, are achieving higher efficiencies at lower production costs. This makes the technology more accessible, particularly in regions with high demand for sustainable energy solutions, such as urban areas and remote rural communities (Alves, 2019).

Furthermore, Silva et al. (2020) note that building-integrated photovoltaic (BIPV) systems are gaining prominence. These systems allow solar cells to be directly incorporated into building facades and rooftops, maximizing the available space for electricity generation. This approach not only enhances the energy efficiency of buildings but also provides an aesthetic and functional solution for decentralized energy generation.

However, the efficiency of photovoltaic systems can be affected by factors such as temperature. As Rabelo (2022) observes, excessively high temperatures can reduce the performance of photovoltaic cells, necessitating the use of power optimizers to minimize losses and ensure efficient generation under adverse climatic conditions. This is an especially relevant challenge in tropical regions, where high temperatures are common.

In summary, the operation of photovoltaic solar systems is based on simple but effective principles for converting sunlight into electricity. Recent technological advances are expanding the possibilities for applying these systems at various scales, from residential installations to large solar power plants.

The next chapter, "Global Expansion of Photovoltaic Energy: Data and Growth Worldwide," will explore the impacts of this growth on the global energy landscape, highlighting the leading countries in adopting this technology and the challenges to be overcome for its large-scale implementation.

## 4.2 THE GLOBAL EXPANSION OF PHOTOVOLTAIC ENERGY: DATA AND GROWTH WORLDWIDE

Photovoltaic solar energy has been expanding globally, establishing itself as one of the leading renewable alternatives for electricity generation. With a significant reduction in installation costs and the implementation of favorable public policies, many countries have experienced exponential growth in installed solar energy capacity.

According to Ahmed et al. (2023), the global installed capacity of photovoltaic solar energy has increased significantly in recent decades, reaching 1,046 GW in 2022. This growth has been primarily driven by massive investments in countries like China, which alone accounts for nearly 37% of the global capacity.

This trend reflects the accelerating adoption of solar technologies, which have become more affordable and efficient, enabling nations such as India and the United States to also emerge as major players in this sector. This development underscores the importance of continuing to support policies that facilitate new solar energy projects on a global scale (Ahmed et al., 2023).

Despite this progress, Filiz-Baştürk (2024) argues that Europe continues to serve as a model of leadership in solar energy use, particularly under the framework of the European Green Deal. The region, historically a pioneer in adopting renewable energy sources, is now intensifying its efforts to further increase the share of solar energy in its energy mix. Countries such as Germany and Spain have been standout performers, while other European Union nations still face regulatory barriers and economic challenges that hinder their ability to keep pace with this expansion. This highlights that while solar energy growth is significant, it remains uneven across different regions of the world.

Complementing this analysis, Gabriel and Silva (2023) highlight that Brazil has experienced remarkable growth in its installed solar energy capacity, which surpassed 32 GW in 2023. Distributed generation, particularly in rural areas and regions with limited access to the electrical grid, has been a key driver of this progress. Supported by public policies such as energy auctions and tax incentives, Brazil has become one of the most promising markets for solar energy in Latin America. However, to sustain this growth, it will be essential to improve infrastructure and integrate solar energy more effectively into the national energy matrix.

Kumar and Ragavendran (2023) argue that the competitiveness of solar energy compared to other renewable sources, such as wind energy, is one of the key factors driving its adoption in many countries. The decline in installation costs and advancements in technologies such as solar trackers have increased the efficiency of photovoltaic systems, making them increasingly attractive for large-scale industrial projects. Moreover, these technological innovations contribute to the economic viability of solar energy, particularly in regions that previously relied exclusively on fossil fuels.

However, Pourasl and Barenji (2023) highlight that significant challenges still hinder the expansion of solar energy, particularly in regions like Africa and parts of Asia. The lack of adequate infrastructure and high initial implementation costs remain substantial obstacles for many developing countries.

Despite these barriers, these countries hold immense potential for adopting solar energy, especially in areas with high solar radiation. This underscores the need for greater international support and accessible financing mechanisms (Pourasl; Barenji, 2023).

In conclusion, the global expansion of photovoltaic energy is reshaping the energy sector, offering a viable and sustainable solution for electricity generation. The rapid growth of this technology in countries like China, the United States, and Brazil, alongside the challenges faced by other regions, demonstrates that solar energy has the potential to become one of the leading energy sources in the coming decades.

## 4.3 TECHNOLOGICAL INNOVATIONS IN PHOTOVOLTAIC CELLS: NEW GENERATIONS AND MATERIALS

The evolution of photovoltaic cells has been marked by significant technological advancements, particularly in the development of new generations and materials that enhance efficiency and reduce production costs. The pursuit of these innovations has been driven by the growing need for sustainable energy sources and competition in the global energy market.

According to Xiao et al. (2023), the use of materials such as nitride carbide in the construction of photovoltaic cells has led to significant advancements in energy conversion efficiency. This material offers high stability and reduced costs, making it a promising candidate for the next generation of solar panels. Although challenges, such as electron-hole pair recombination, continue to limit its efficiency, innovative surface modification strategies have shown potential to improve the performance of these devices.

Moreover, Chen et al. (2023) highlight that the doping of graphene in van der Waals heterostructures is a groundbreaking innovation in the field of solar cells. Graphene, due to its exceptional electrical conductivity and mechanical flexibility, has been integrated into silicon photovoltaic cells to enhance electron collection efficiency. This combination of materials has enabled the development of more efficient and cost-effective cells, broadening the commercial viability of these technologies, particularly for large-scale applications.

Another significant advancement is the use of perovskite solar cells, which have seen an exponential increase in scientific publications, reflecting growing academic and industrial interest. Perovskite cells, with efficiencies exceeding 25%, are among the most promising technologies to replace silicon as the primary photovoltaic material. However, the instability of these materials under adverse environmental conditions remains a challenge that must be addressed for large-scale adoption (Braga et al., 2023).

According to Ferreira and Pacheco (2023), another notable innovation in the photovoltaic field is the use of ultrathin photovoltaic films, which offer greater versatility and ease of installation due to their lightweight and flexible nature. These films can be applied in locations where traditional panels are not feasible, such as building facades and the roofs of electric vehicles. The ability to incorporate this technology into diverse surfaces opens new possibilities for energy generation in urban environments, reducing the reliance on large areas for solar panel installation.

The development of hybrid materials, such as nitrogen-doped carbon compounds, has also been critical in improving photovoltaic conversion capabilities. These materials combine high thermal and electrical conductivity with photothermal properties, resulting in solar cells that are both more efficient and more stable. The use of these compounds in conjunction with traditional technologies allows for significant increases in energy efficiency without substantially raising production costs (Le et al., 2023).

In conclusion, technological innovations in photovoltaic cells continue to advance, with new materials and generations of cells showing tremendous potential to drive the efficiency and accessibility of this renewable energy source. The next chapter will explore the integration of solar energy into power grids: challenges and opportunities, analyzing how these innovations can be implemented within existing energy grids and addressing both the benefits and the challenges of this integration.

## 4.4 INTEGRATION OF SOLAR ENERGY INTO POWER GRIDS: CHALLENGES AND OPPORTUNITIES

The integration of solar energy into power grids has emerged as one of the most promising yet challenging aspects of the global energy transition. With the increasing adoption of photovoltaic systems within electricity distribution and transmission networks, technological innovations and new management models are essential to ensure the efficiency, reliability, and stability of energy supply.

According to Barreto (2023), one of the biggest challenges in integrating solar energy is related to reverse power flow, which occurs when energy generated by photovoltaic systems is injected back into the distribution grid. This phenomenon can cause voltage fluctuations and other power quality issues, particularly in areas with high concentrations of installed photovoltaic systems. Solutions such as the use of smart inverters and real-time control systems are being explored to mitigate these effects, ensuring the safe and stable operation of the grid.

Furthermore, as noted by Vishwakarma et al. (2024), the role of power electronic converters is critical to the efficiency and reliability of grid-connected photovoltaic systems. These devices are responsible for converting the direct current (DC) generated by solar panels into alternating current (AC), which is compatible with electrical grids.

Advanced converter technologies, such as multi-level converters, have shown significant potential in improving integration efficiency by reducing harmonic distortions and optimizing energy flow. This underscores the importance of investing in technological innovations to ensure compatibility between electrical grids and renewable energy sources (Vishwakarma et al., 2024).

On the other hand, the intermittency of solar generation presents another major challenge, as emphasized by Bislimi and Nikaj (2023). The variability of solar generation, driven by climate changes and daily cycles, can compromise grid stability. To address this, energy storage systems and demand management strategies are required to balance electricity supply and consumption. The integration of battery storage and the development of smart grids are essential to managing these fluctuations, providing greater flexibility and resilience to the electrical system.

Menzri et al. (2024) point out that the use of advanced control techniques, such as Sliding Mode Control (SMC) and Direct Power Control (DPC), has proven effective in integrating solar energy into power grids. These methodologies enable real-time adjustments to photovoltaic energy generation, optimizing the maximum power point and minimizing losses during energy injection into the grid.

According to the authors, the result is greater operational efficiency and improved adaptation of solar generation to the demands of the electrical system, contributing to grid stability (Menzri et al., 2024).

Additionally, the integration of hybrid systems that combine solar and wind energy can also serve as an efficient solution to the challenges of intermittency. The combination of these complementary sources helps reduce the variability of renewable energy generation, as the output of one source can compensate for the lower output of the other. This hybrid approach provides a more reliable and cost-effective solution for large-scale renewable energy integration, especially in regions with variable climatic conditions (Al Badwawi et al., 2015).

In conclusion, the integration of solar energy into power grids presents both significant challenges and opportunities for the future of renewable energy. Key factors include energy conversion technologies, advanced control systems, and the integration of hybrid solutions to ensure the efficiency and stability of electrical systems.

The next chapter will explore "Economic Aspects: Cost-Benefit and Incentives for Solar Energy Adoption," analyzing how economic factors and incentive policies have driven the adoption of photovoltaic systems in different regions of the world. The chapter will highlight the importance of economic incentives in facilitating the energy transition.

## 4.5 ECONOMIC ASPECTS: COST-BENEFIT AND INCENTIVES FOR SOLAR ENERGY ADOPTION

The adoption of photovoltaic solar energy has been widely discussed in the context of economic benefits and incentives, considering the high initial costs and the long-term environmental advantages. One of solar energy's main appeals is its ability to significantly reduce electricity costs across various scales, from residential properties to large institutions.

According to Silva and Amaral (2023), an analysis of the feasibility of a residential photovoltaic system revealed that, despite the high initial cost, long-term savings—especially with attractive financing options—justify the implementation of this technology. By analyzing scenarios, such as financing plans of up to 60 installments, it was shown that significant reductions in electricity bills could be achieved, making the investment economically advantageous.

Another study, conducted at Christus College in Piauí, also confirmed the economic viability of implementing a photovoltaic system. A project designed to meet the institution's energy demands demonstrated a relatively short financial payback period, establishing itself as a sustainable and economically efficient solution. This example underscores the importance of evaluating not only installation costs but also energy consumption and future demand to maximize the return on investment (Silva et al., 2023).

There is also the example of companies like Natura, which installed solar panels at its headquarters, further illustrating how the use of renewable energy can not only reduce operational costs but also generate positive environmental impacts. A study by Arigony et al. (2024) highlights that, in addition to economic viability, the project significantly reduced $CO_2$ emissions, aligning with the company's strategic goals and reinforcing its sustainability practices.

From a technical perspective, the use of hybrid systems, as discussed by Ijeoma et al. (2024), presents an interesting approach for regions with less stable electrical infrastructure. For example, in Nigeria, the adoption of a hybrid solar-battery-generator system resulted in a significant reduction in the cost per kWh and demonstrated a rapid financial payback. This makes it an attractive option from both economic and environmental standpoints.

Additionally, Zublie et al. (2023) examined the impact of public policies promoting solar energy, such as the Net Energy Metering (NEM) program in Malaysia. This incentive allows consumers to sell excess energy generated back to the grid, providing an additional financial return. Their analysis revealed that, over a 21-year period, the cumulative savings for an institution adopting NEM would be substantial, along with a significant reduction in $CO_2$ emissions.

Adamu (2015) emphasizes that although Africa's solar potential is immense, many countries are still in the early stages of adopting solar technologies. The author highlights the need for more robust policies to encourage the use of solar energy and to make projects economically viable, particularly in rural areas. This includes measures such as reducing initial costs and creating subsidies to promote the adoption of this technology.

Thus, it can be concluded that the economic aspects of adopting solar energy, such as cost-benefit analyses and incentives, are critical to the success of the energy transition. The analysis of the cases mentioned demonstrates that, despite the high initial investment, the long-term financial benefits, combined with governmental incentives, make solar energy a viable and sustainable solution.

# 5 INNOVATIONS AND TECHNOLOGICAL SOLUTIONS IN DISTRIBUTED ENERGY GENERATION

The global energy transition is deeply tied to the adoption of new technologies that enhance efficiency and sustainability in energy generation and distribution. In this context, distributed energy generation has emerged as a central concept, redefining how electricity is produced and consumed.

This study will explore the main features of this model, its benefits, and the global trends shaping its expansion. Additionally, it will analyze the role of hybrid and integrated systems that combine different renewable energy sources, such as solar and wind, to optimize the use of natural resources and maximize energy efficiency.

Another key focus will be the increasing digitalization of energy management, driven by the advent of the Internet of Things (IoT) and smart platforms, which are transforming how energy systems are monitored and controlled. New products and business models in the solar sector will also be discussed, highlighting innovative cases that are redefining the energy market. The challenges and opportunities presented by distributed generation will be examined, showcasing how this model can accelerate both the decarbonization and democratization of energy.

# 5.1 DISTRIBUTED ENERGY GENERATION: CONCEPT AND GLOBAL OVERVIEW

Distributed energy generation (DG) has been steadily emerging as a strategic solution in the global energy transition, promoting the decentralization of electricity supply and increasing the resilience of energy systems. With the growing demand for renewable energy sources and the need to reduce reliance on fossil fuels, DG enables individual consumers and communities to generate their own energy while connecting to the power grid in an efficient and sustainable manner.

This chapter will examine the fundamental concepts of DG, addressing its role in the global energy landscape and highlighting the opportunities and challenges this technology faces in different regions.

DG is characterized by the generation of energy close to the point of consumption, reducing losses associated with transmitting electricity over long distances. As explained by Gasparin and Bühler (2018), one of the primary advantages of this model is the diversification of the energy mix, which is particularly important in countries like Brazil, where dependence on a single energy source, such as hydropower, can lead to vulnerabilities during periods of water scarcity.

Moreover, the integration of renewable sources such as photovoltaic solar energy has significantly expanded the adoption of DG in various parts of the world, making energy systems more sustainable and accessible (Gasparin; Bühler, 2018).

Another key aspect, as discussed by Ananduta and Ocampo-Martinez (2019), is the economic efficiency DG can provide. The use of microgrids and distributed storage systems, for example, offers greater flexibility in energy management and enables communities to become self-sufficient. This not only enhances energy resilience in these regions but also reduces energy costs, benefiting remote or hard-to-reach areas in particular.

Globally, DG is being driven by a combination of technological advancements and favorable regulatory policies. According to Córdova-González et al. (2024), many countries have adopted interconnection standards and incentive policies to promote renewable distributed generation, making it easier to connect these systems to the grid. However, challenges persist, particularly in regions with weak energy infrastructure or insufficient incentive policies to attract significant investments.

In this context, Ciriminna et al. (2018) highlight the importance of synergy between distributed generation (DG) policies and environmental sustainability initiatives. The growth of distributed generation, particularly through renewable sources, not only contributes to reducing greenhouse gas emissions but also promotes social inclusion by enabling isolated communities to access a reliable and clean energy source. This underscores the role of DG as a crucial tool in combating climate change and fostering a more equitable and just energy transition.

On the other hand, Getahun (2021) points out that the expansion of DG also faces significant challenges, one of the main obstacles being the integration of these systems into conventional power grids, which were not originally designed to handle the intermittency and variability of renewable energy sources. The development of control technologies, such as smart inverters and real-time monitoring systems, will be essential to overcoming these challenges and ensuring grid stability.

In conclusion, distributed generation represents a unique opportunity to transform the global energy sector by promoting a transition to renewable sources and decentralizing electricity production.

However, for this transition to succeed, coordinated efforts among governments, businesses, and communities are necessary, along with continuous investments in technology and infrastructure.

## 5.2 INNOVATIVE CASES: NEW PRODUCTS AND BUSINESS MODELS IN THE SOLAR ENERGY SECTOR

The solar energy sector has become a hub for significant innovations, driven by both technological advancements and new business models. It is crucial to examine examples of innovative products and business strategies that are reshaping the solar energy market, as the adoption of emerging technologies, combined with the pursuit of sustainability, has created new opportunities for businesses and consumers alike.

The development of new solar energy storage technologies, such as more efficient lithium batteries and advanced control systems, has facilitated the integration of this energy source into power grids. Long et al. (2023) emphasize that innovation in business models, such as the combination of "renewable energy + storage," has proven essential for stabilizing grids and increasing the share of renewable energy in the global energy mix. These technologies allow companies to offer more effective solutions, reducing the volatility of solar energy generation and improving system reliability.

In addition to technological innovations, new business models have gained prominence, particularly in the context of energy communities and peer-to-peer energy trading. These models allow consumers and small-scale solar energy producers to trade electricity directly, without the need for traditional intermediaries. This creates a more decentralized and efficient ecosystem, which has attracted the interest of investors and consumers seeking greater energy independence and a more collaborative model of energy management (Karami, 2024).

Moreover, cooperation between governments, universities, and industry has played a crucial role in fostering innovation in the solar energy sector. As Gomes et al. (2023) explain, strategic partnerships, such as the "triple helix" model, are essential for the development of advanced technologies and the implementation of innovative solutions in the market.

These collaborations have enabled the creation of new tools, such as artificial intelligence systems that assist in monitoring and optimizing solar power plants, improving operational efficiency and reducing costs (Gomes et al., 2023).

Mori and Zhang (2024) further explain that a key driver behind the development of new products and business models in the solar energy sector is government incentives and public policies that support innovation. Creating an innovation-friendly environment, with policies that encourage both research and the development of new technologies, has been crucial to the success of major initiatives in the sector.

These incentives enable companies and research institutions to continue developing more efficient and sustainable solutions for the solar energy market.

In addition to government incentives, Rinto et al. (2024) highlight that the digitalization of the sector has been a driving force for innovation. The combination of photovoltaic technologies with smart grids has the potential to optimize the use of solar energy, integrating it more effectively into distribution networks. These technologies allow for real-time monitoring and dynamic adjustment of energy supply and demand, promoting more efficient use of renewable resources.

Thus, new products and business models in the solar energy sector represent a significant transformation in how energy is generated and consumed. It is crucial to understand the challenges and opportunities of distributed generation for the energy transition, a highly relevant topic for ensuring the sustainable expansion of renewable energy sources.

## 5.3 MOBILE ENERGY: TECHNOLOGICAL INNOVATIONS IN DISTRIBUTED AND VIRTUAL SOLAR ENERGY GENERATION

### 5.3.1 Remote and Virtual Solar Energy Generation: Optimizing Access to Renewable Energy

Renewable energy generation, particularly solar energy, has rapidly advanced worldwide, driven by the pursuit of more sustainable and accessible energy sources. However, one of the challenges many consumers face is the inability to install solar panels on their own homes or businesses, whether due to space limitations, unsuitable climatic conditions, or financial constraints. In this context, innovations such as remote and virtual solar energy generation have emerged as a solution, enabling participation in the renewable energy market without the need for physical on-site installation.

This concept, exemplified by the Energia Móvel system, provides a viable alternative for consumers interested in acquiring virtual solar panels connected to photovoltaic plants, maximizing access to renewable energy in a practical and efficient way.

The Energia Móvel system facilitates remote energy generation by connecting consumers to physical solar panels installed in solar farms through a digital platform. Through this technology, consumers can purchase a "virtual panel," which corresponds to a physical panel installed in a plant. This ensures that even without the need for local infrastructure to install panels, consumers can benefit from solar energy generation by receiving energy credits equivalent to what would have been generated at their own property. This innovation expands access to renewable energy for densely populated urban areas or regions where physical installation would be unfeasible.

In addition to the convenience offered by remote generation, this model allows for the direct integration of energy credits generated at the solar farm into the local electricity distributor's energy compensation system. Consumers can receive credits on their electricity bills or even monetize the energy production through direct transfers to their bank accounts. This process not only democratizes access to clean energy but also encourages the adoption of renewable sources by transforming solar energy into a tangible and accessible financial asset.

Another notable aspect of the system is the flexibility it offers in terms of scalability. Consumers can acquire as many virtual panels as they wish, adjusting the volume of energy generated to meet their consumption needs. This makes the model viable for a wide range of users, from residential consumers to small and large businesses.

This level of customization also ensures that consumers can expand their energy generation capacity as their energy demands grow. Additionally, the system is fully monitored and operated remotely, eliminating the need for direct maintenance by the user.

The following Figure 1 illustrates how the remote and virtual solar energy generation system functions, detailing the steps from the acquisition of the virtual panel to its connection with the physical panel installed at the solar farm, as well as real-time tracking of energy production.

Figure 1 – Functionality of the Remote and Virtual Solar Energy Generation System

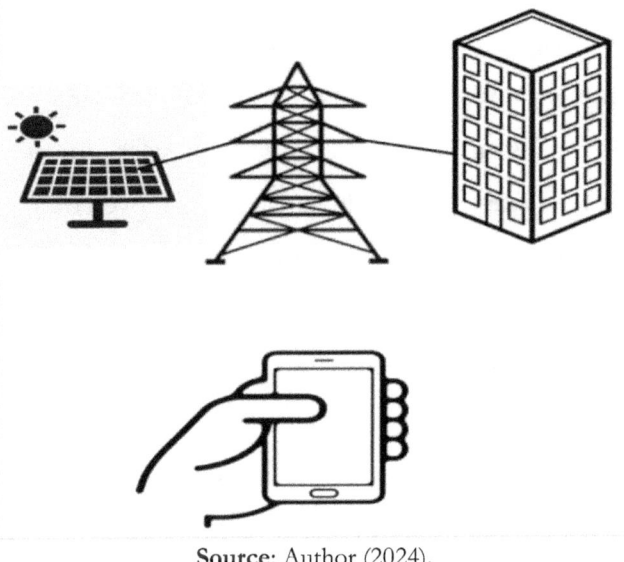

Source: Author (2024).

Another critical factor for the success of remote generation is the use of advanced digital technologies. Through apps and online platforms, users can monitor the energy production of their virtual panels in real time, making it easier to manage their participation in the solar energy market.

These platforms provide a user-friendly and accessible interface, simplifying the monitoring process for consumers who may lack technical knowledge about energy generation. Illustrations from the Application Presentation materials can be used to demonstrate this functionality, offering a clear visualization of how to virtually manage energy production.

Beyond the individual benefits, the remote generation model also promotes large-scale sustainability. By enabling more consumers to participate in clean energy generation, this system contributes to the expansion of solar farms and the reduction of the carbon footprint associated with traditional power grids. Decentralizing energy production further strengthens the resilience of the electrical grid by distributing generation across multiple points and reducing reliance on large, centralized power plants. The model proposed by Energia Móvel thus benefits consumers directly while also enhancing the overall energy sector.

In conclusion, remote and virtual solar energy generation represents an innovative and effective solution for overcoming barriers to renewable energy access, democratizing adoption and providing direct economic benefits to consumers. In this context, it is essential to understand how real-time monitoring and the monetization of energy production are facilitated by digital platforms that interconnect these virtual panels. This underscores the importance of these technologies in ensuring the efficient and transparent operation of the system.

## 5.3.2 Real-Time Monitoring Systems and Energy Production Monetization

Advances in digital technologies have significantly transformed the energy sector, particularly in the realm of distributed generation and real-time management. One of the most notable developments in this transformation is the ability to remotely monitor energy production, providing consumers with greater control and transparency.

Among the most remarkable innovations, the Energia Móvel system offers a revolutionary solution by combining solar energy generation with a real-time monitoring platform and an efficient monetization model. This system enables consumers to track the energy production of their virtual solar panels, optimizing energy use and ensuring financial returns, thereby reshaping the energy sector with an innovative and accessible approach to distributed generation.

Through the Energia Móvel platform, users can monitor in real time the amount of energy generated by their virtual solar panels, which are remotely connected to solar farms. This functionality gives consumers full control over their energy production, allowing them to instantly view the performance of their panels and adjust consumption according to generation levels.

The innovation of this system lies in its ability to seamlessly integrate energy generation and monitoring, offering a unique user experience. Consumers can optimize their energy use and increase efficiency without requiring specialized technical knowledge.

In addition to monitoring, Energia Móvel allows consumers to receive notifications and alerts about panel performance, enabling them to take preventive or corrective actions when necessary. This significantly enhances system reliability and provides users with peace of mind, supported by a continuous flow of information about their energy production. Furthermore, the platform's user-friendly interface makes it easy to visualize data, ensuring the system is intuitive and accessible to all types of consumers.

One of the most innovative aspects of Energia Móvel is the ability to monetize the energy generated. The system allows excess energy produced by virtual panels to be converted into credits on the consumer's energy bill or, alternatively, into monetary values that can be transferred directly to the user's bank account.

This functionality not only reduces electricity costs but also transforms solar energy production into a source of income, creating a new economic model in which the energy generated by consumers holds direct financial value.

The combination of real-time monitoring and energy production monetization provides a significant competitive advantage in the solar energy market, positioning Energia Móvel as an innovative and highly attractive solution for consumers of all profiles. Small energy producers, for example, can actively participate in the market, leveraging the financial benefits of surplus energy generation while contributing to the broader energy transition. The system's flexibility and scalability allow it to adapt to both residential and large-scale business applications, promoting the democratization of access to renewable energy.

In addition to being an economically advantageous solution, Energia Móvel encourages conscious energy consumption. Real-time monitoring offers valuable insights into generation and consumption patterns, enabling users to adjust their habits to maximize solar energy use. This not only increases system efficiency but also reduces reliance on non-renewable energy sources, reinforcing a commitment to environmental sustainability.

Thus, Energia Móvel represents a revolution in the solar energy sector by combining real-time monitoring with an innovative monetization model. In this context, it is important to understand the opportunities for energy and financial inclusion enabled by digital platforms and how solutions like Energia Móvel are expanding access to renewable energy while creating new opportunities for market participation for a wider range of consumers.

### 5.3.3 Opportunities for Energy and Financial Inclusion Through Digital Platforms

Digital platforms have revolutionized the energy sector, creating new opportunities for both consumer inclusion in the energy market and income generation through renewable sources. These innovations promote the democratization of access to clean energy, enabling individuals and businesses that previously could not participate in energy generation to do so efficiently and economically.

One of the main opportunities brought by digital platforms is the inclusion of consumers in locations where the physical installation of renewable energy systems would be unfeasible. Thanks to systems like Energia Móvel, consumers can purchase virtual solar panels, connecting to distant solar farms and generating energy credits without the need for local infrastructure. This innovation allows individuals and businesses to enter the distributed generation market regardless of their geographic or structural conditions. The transformative aspect of this model lies in enabling everyone to access the benefits of renewable energy generation without the traditional physical barriers.

Additionally, digital platforms simplify the process of monitoring and managing energy production. Through intuitive apps, consumers can track the amount of energy generated, monitor the performance of their panels, and adjust their consumption based on real-time data.

This level of transparency and control allows users to optimize their energy generation and consumption, maximizing both economic and environmental benefits. By facilitating continuous monitoring, digital platforms ensure that consumers actively participate in managing their energy production.

Another important aspect is the monetization of surplus energy generated, which can be converted into credits on the energy bill or even direct financial returns. This functionality, offered by systems like Energia Móvel, transforms solar energy production into an investment opportunity, where consumers can earn income by generating more energy than they consume.

This model not only reduces energy costs but also encourages the use of renewable sources as an additional source of income, integrating consumers into the energy market in an unprecedented way.

Digital platforms also enable the creation of new business models in the energy sector, with energy communities and peer-to-peer energy networks emerging as viable solutions thanks to digital technology. In this model, consumers can share or sell surplus energy directly to other consumers, creating a more dynamic and decentralized ecosystem. This approach fosters collaboration among users and encourages the development of local networks for energy generation and consumption, further enhancing energy inclusion.

Beyond financial and operational benefits, digital platforms also promote social inclusion and sustainability. By enabling entire communities—particularly in remote or low-income areas—to access renewable energy affordably, these platforms play a crucial role in reducing energy inequality. Initiatives that facilitate access to solar energy through digital platforms directly contribute to the global energy transition by expanding access to clean and sustainable energy for a larger portion of the population.

In conclusion, digital platforms are transforming how energy is generated, consumed, and monetized, creating new opportunities for energy and financial inclusion. Through these innovations, consumers who were previously excluded from the energy market can now actively participate, generating their own energy, monitoring its performance, and turning surplus energy into a source of income.

# 6 CONCLUSION

The conclusion of this study aimed to consolidate the analysis of the role of photovoltaic energy in the global energy transition, emphasizing the importance of this technology in the context of sustainability and distributed generation. Throughout the study, the main challenges related to dependence on fossil fuels and their implications for global warming were discussed, as well as emerging trends toward a cleaner and more efficient energy matrix. The progress of public policies and international agreements has played a critical role in promoting the development of renewable energy sources, such as solar energy, and the growing awareness surrounding a low-carbon economy points to a scenario of global transformation.

The global energy transition faces considerable obstacles, such as legacy infrastructure reliant on fossil fuels, which requires significant economic and political restructuring. The analysis demonstrated that despite the goals set by agreements such as the Paris Agreement, dependence on oil, gas, and coal persists in many economies, delaying the adoption of renewable energy. However, future trends indicate an acceleration of this transition, driven in particular by the decreasing costs of photovoltaic technologies and the advancement of fiscal and financial incentive policies.

The fundamentals of photovoltaic solar energy, discussed in this study, reveal the simplicity and efficiency of this system in converting solar radiation into electricity. However, the study highlighted that large-scale adoption still faces challenges, such as the intermittency of solar generation and the need for integration into traditional power grids. The global expansion of this technology, supported by innovations in materials and new types of photovoltaic cells, such as perovskite cells, has contributed to improving its efficiency, making solar energy an increasingly viable solution to meet contemporary energy demands.

In the field of distributed generation, technological innovations have played a fundamental role in decentralizing energy production. New products and business models, such as microgrid systems and digital platforms that enable energy production monetization, are transforming the way energy is generated and consumed. The energy inclusion facilitated by these innovations has the potential to democratize access to solar energy, allowing individuals and businesses to actively participate in the distributed generation market, even in areas where the installation of photovoltaic systems would otherwise be unfeasible.

While this study has explored in detail the technological innovations and opportunities for solar energy expansion, some limitations should be acknowledged. The research was predominantly bibliographic, which limits the analysis of empirical data and specific cases of implementation in different regional contexts. Future research could benefit from field studies and a deeper analysis of the socioeconomic impact of adopting photovoltaic technologies in rural and urban communities in developing countries.

The importance of photovoltaic energy for the energy transition and global sustainability is undeniable, as evidenced throughout this study. Its contributions go beyond reducing greenhouse gas emissions to include creating new markets and opportunities for financial inclusion. With the advancement of monitoring technologies and the adoption of distributed generation models, solar energy is becoming a cornerstone of the transition toward a low-carbon economy, directly contributing to mitigating the impacts of climate change.

In summary, this study reinforces the argument that photovoltaic solar energy, driven by technological innovations and emerging business models, plays a central role in transforming the energy sector. Its expansion, combined with the development of robust public policies and the use of digital platforms to promote energy inclusion, has the potential to redefine the future of energy matrices worldwide, fostering a more equitable, sustainable, and efficient transition.

# REFERÊNCIAS

ADAMU, Abubakar. Harnessing the solar energy for economic development in Africa. **Advances in Economics and Business Management (AEBM)**, v. 2, n. 6, p. 660-671, abr./jun. 2015. Disponível em: https://www.academia.edu/download/100162275/04Jul2015040706z21_20_20_20_20_20_20_20_20Abubakar_20Adamu_____20_20_20660-671.pdf. Acesso em: 07 ago. 2024.

AHMED, Raghad *et al.* **A review paper on current state of the worldwide solar energy generation.** In: E3S Web of Conferences. EDP Sciences, 2024. p. 01079. Disponível em: https://www.e3s-conferences.org/articles/e3sconf/pdf/2024/37/e3sconf_icftest2024_01079.pdf. Acesso em: 09 ago. 2024.

AKAEV, Askar A.; DAVYDOVA, Olga I. Mathematical description of energy transition scenarios based on the latest technologies and trends. **Energies**, v. 14, n. 24, p. 8360, 2021. Disponível em: https://www.mdpi.com/1996-1073/14/24/8360/pdf. Acesso em: 04 ago. 2024.

AL BADWAWI, Rashid; ABUSARA, Mohammad; MALLICK, Tapas. A review of hybrid solar PV and wind energy system. **Smart Science**, v. 3, n. 3, p. 127-138, 2015. Disponível em: https://www.tandfonline.com/doi/pdf/10.1080/23080477.2015.11665647. Acesso em: 09 ago. 2024.

ALVES, Marliana de Oliveira Lage. **Energia solar**: estudo da geração de energia elétrica através dos sistemas fotovoltaicos on-grid e off-grid. Trabalho de Conclusão de Curso (Bacharelado em Engenharia Elétrica) – Instituto de Ciências Exatas e Aplicadas, Universidade Federal de Ouro Preto, João Monlevade, 2019. Disponível em: http://monografias.ufop.br/bitstream/35400000/2019/6/MONOGRAFIA_EnergiaSolarEstudo.pdf. Acesso em: 08 ago. 2024.

ANNAMALAI, Kalyan; THANAPAL, Siva Sankar; RANJAN, Devesh. Ranking renewable and fossil fuels on global warming potential using respiratory quotient concept. ***Journal of Combustion***, v. 2018, n. 1, p. 1270708, 2018. Disponível em:

https://onlinelibrary.wiley.com/doi/pdf/10.1155/2018/1270708. Acesso em: 03 ago. 2024.

ARIGONY, Ana Luiza *et al*. Avaliação econômico-financeira da implementação de energia solar na sede da Natura: viabilidade e impactos sustentáveis. **Revista de Gestão e Secretariado**, v. 15, n. 8, p. e4075-e4075, 2024. Disponível em: https://ojs.revistagesec.org.br/secretariado/article/download/4075/2663. Acesso em: 09 ago. 2024.

BARRETO, Ikaro Teles Bezerra dos Santos. **Análise das implicações do uso da energia solar fotovoltaica na rede de distribuição**. Trabalho de Conclusão de Curso (Bacharelado em Engenharia de Energia) – Universidade Federal de Alagoas, Campus CECA, Rio Largo, AL, 2023. Disponível em: https://www.repositorio.ufal.br/jspui/bitstream/123456789/13932/1/An%C3%A1lise%20das%20implica%C3%A7%C3%B5es%20do%20uso%20da%20energia%20solar%20fotovoltaica%20na%20rede%20de%20distribui%C3%A7%C3%A3o.pdf. Acesso em: 07 ago. 2024.

BAZILIAN, Morgan *et al*. Four scenarios of the energy transition: drivers, consequences, and implications for geopolitics. **Wiley Interdisciplinary Reviews: Climate Change**, v. 11, n. 2, p. e625, 2020. Disponível em: https://wrap.warwick.ac.uk/133545/1/WRAP-four-scenarios-energy-transition-Bradshaw-2019.pdf. Acesso em: 12 ago. 2024.

BENTO, Nuno; BORELLO, Mattia; GIANFRATE, Gianfranco. Market-pull policies to promote renewable energy: a quantitative assessment of tendering implementation. **Journal of Cleaner Production**, v. 248, p. 119209, 2020. Disponível em: https://repositorio.iscte-iul.pt/bitstream/10071/20143/1/Accepted%20Manuscript.pdf. Acesso em: 08 ago. 2024.

BISLIMI, Agron; NIKAJ, Arbesa. **Analyzing solar energy integration in smart grids with a focus on demand response, energy management, and grid stability**. 2023. Disponível em: https://www.researchgate.net/profile/Agron-Bislimi/publication/377952692_Analyzing_Solar_Energy_Integration_in_Smart_Grids_with_a_Focus_on_Demand_Response_Energy_Management_and_Grid_Stability/links/65be8043790074549761b5ee/Analyzing

-Solar-Energy-Integration-in-Smart-Grids-with-a-Focus-on-Demand-Response-Energy-Management-and-Grid-Stability.pdf. Acesso em: 05 ago. 2024.

BLASIO, Nicola; ZHENG, Derek. The future of energy value chains in the transition to a low-carbon economy: an evaluation framework of integration and segmentation scenarios. **Environment and Natural Resources Program & Science, Technology, and Public Policy Program Papers**, 2023. Disponível em: https://dash.harvard.edu/bitstream/handle/1/37376806/De%20Blasio%20Zheng_Energy%20Value%20Chains_FINAL.pdf?sequence=1. Acesso em: 03 ago. 2024.

BRAGA, Marcelo Rocha *et al*. **Análise bibliométrica das inovações em tecnologias de geração de energia solar na base Scopus.** In: Anais Congresso Brasileiro de Energia Solar-CBENS, 2024. Disponível em: https://anaiscbens.emnuvens.com.br/cbens/article/download/2335/2325. Acesso em: 05 ago. 2024.

BREYER, Christian *et al*. Reflecting the energy transition from a European perspective and in the global context—relevance of solar photovoltaics benchmarking two ambitious scenarios. **Progress in Photovoltaics: Research and Applications**, v. 31, n. 12, p. 1369-1395, 2023. Disponível em: https://onlinelibrary.wiley.com/doi/pdfdirect/10.1002/pip.3659. Acesso em: 02 ago. 2024.

BRIGIDO, Caroline R. *et al*. **Lítio**: um elemento estratégico para uma economia de baixo carbono. 2023. 4 al 6 de Octubre de 2023. Salta, Argentina. XVI Jornadas Argentinas de Tratamiento de Minerales. Disponível em: http://master.cetem.gov.br/bitstream/cetem/3716/3/CAC00230023%20L%C3%ADtio%20Um%20Elemento%20Estrat%C3%A9gico%20para%20uma%20Economia%20de%20Baixo%20Carbono-5.pdf. Acesso em: 12 ago. 2024.

CARVALHO, Micaele Martins; MAGALHÃES, Aline Souza; DOMINGUES, Edson Paulo. **Economia de baixo carbono no Brasil: custos setoriais e potenciais de abatimento**. Disponível em: https://brsa.org.br/wp-content/uploads/wpcf7-submissions/7126/identificado.pdf. Acesso em: 07 ago. 2024.

CHEN, Xiao et al. Co/N co-doped flower-like carbon-based phase change materials toward solar energy harvesting. **Aggregate**, v. 5, n. 1, p. e413, 2024. Disponível em: https://onlinelibrary.wiley.com/doi/pdf/10.1002/agt2.413. Acesso em: 09 ago. 2024.

CIRIMINNA, Rosaria et al. Expanding the distributed generation concept: toward decentralized energy and water supply. **Global Challenges**, v. 2, n. 4, p. 1800006, 2018. Disponível em: https://onlinelibrary.wiley.com/doi/pdfdirect/10.1002/gch2.201800006. Acesso em: 03 ago. 2024.

DIMITRIEV, Oleg; YOSHIDA, Tsukasa; SUN, He. Principles of solar energy storage. **Energy Storage**, v. 2, n. 1, p. e96, 2020. Disponível em: https://www.researchgate.net/profile/Oleg-Dimitriev/publication/336535768_Principles_of_solar_energy_storage/links/5de5225492851c83645cd9df/Principles-of-solar-energy-storage.pdf. Acesso em: 06 ago. 2024.

FERREIRA, Luiz Felipe de Carvalho; PACHECO, Jonas dos Santos. Novos usos para a energia solar diante das mudanças tecnológicas mundiais. **Revista Ibero-Americana de Humanidades, Ciências e Educação**, v. 8, n. 11, p. 3165-3175, 2022. Disponível em: https://periodicorease.pro.br/rease/article/download/7947/3125. Acesso em: 07 ago. 2024.

GABRIEL, Maycon Eduardo Gonçalves; SILVA, Rogério José José. Inventário: panorama da energia solar no Brasil e no mundo. **Revista dos Trabalhos de Iniciação Científica**, 2023. Disponível em: https://periodicos.unifei.edu.br/index.php/rtic/article/download/536/383. Acesso em: 11 ago. 2024.

GETAHUN, Tayachew Zemenu et al. **Decentralized virtual synchronous generator for the integration of energy storage and distributed generation in the electrical grid**. 2021. Dissertação (Mestrado) – [Instituição não informada]. Disponível em: https://digibuo.uniovi.es/dspace/bitstream/handle/10651/74021/TFM_TayachewZemenuGetahun.pdf?sequence=3. Acesso em: 05 ago. 2024.

GOMES, Amanda Mendes Ferreira et al. Impactos da cooperação governo-universidade-indústria na inovação no setor de energia solar fotovoltaica: estudo de caso. **Revista Brasileira de Energia Solar**, v. 15,

n. 1, p. 64-72, 2024. Disponível em: https://rbens.emnuvens.com.br/rbens/article/download/454/319. Acesso em: 09 ago. 2024.

GUTIERREZ, Maria Bernadete G. P. Sarmiento. **A função do Estado no setor de energia nos países da OCDE**: equilibrando a segurança energética, a eficiência e a sustentabilidade. Brasília: IPEA, jun. 2021. Disponível em: https://www.academia.edu/download/99558094/210708_td_2667.pdf. Acesso em: 12 ago. 2024.

HUNTINGFORD, Chris *et al*. Potential impacts of rapidly changing european use of fossil fuels on global warming. ***Environmental Research Communications***, v. 5, n. 9, p. 091002, 2023. Disponível em: https://iopscience.iop.org/article/10.1088/2515-7620/acf3d7/pdf. Acesso em: 01 ago. 2024.

IJEOMA, Muzan Williams *et al*. Technical, economic, and environmental feasibility assessment of solar-battery-generator hybrid energy systems: a case study in Nigeria. **Frontiers in Energy Research**, v. 12, p. 1397037, 2024. Disponível em: https://www.frontiersin.org/articles/10.3389/fenrg.2024.1397037/pdf. Acesso em: 11 ago. 2024.

INPI – Instituto Nacional da Propriedade Industrial. **Boletim da propriedade Industrial n. 2023/09/12**. 12 set. 2023.

KARAMI, Mahdi. **Driving sustainability through business model innovation in the energy industry and related sectors**. 2024. Tese (Doutorado) – RWTH Aachen University, 2023. Disponível em: https://d-nb.info/134171912X/34. Acesso em: 02 ago. 2024.

KARI, Michael Priesthood. Alleged fossil fuels driven climate change and global warming: evidence proves otherwise. ***AJIEEL***, v. 9, n. 1, p. 183–218, 2024. Disponível em: https://ajieel.com/index.php/a/article/download/93/88. Acesso em: 05 ago. 2024.

KOÇASLAN, Gelengül. Conceptualizing energy efficiency within the scope of energy security and energy sustainability. **Stratejik ve Sosyal Araştırmalar Dergisi**, v. 6, n. 3, p. 581-594, 2022. Disponível em:

https://dergipark.org.tr/en/download/article-file/2651415. Acesso em: 02 ago. 2024.

KUMAR, P.; RAGAVENDRAN, S. **Observing the worldwide advancement of renewable electricity while evaluating the significance of solar energy**. 2023. Disponível em: https://ijnres.org/wp-content/uploads/2024/02/ijnres_ddddd-2.pdf. Acesso em: 05 ago. 2024.

LE, Top Khac *et al*. Advances in solar energy harvesting integrated by van der Waals graphene heterojunctions. **RSC Advances**, v. 13, n. 44, p. 31273-31291, 2023. Disponível em: https://pubs.rsc.org/en/content/articlepdf/2023/ra/d3ra06016k. Acesso em: 11 ago. 2024.

LONG, Fei *et al*. **'Renewable energy+ energy storage' business model innovation--an emerging sustainable business model innovation**. In: SHS Web of Conferences. EDP Sciences, 2023. p. 02007. Disponível em: https://www.shs-conferences.org/articles/shsconf/pdf/2023/12/shsconf_icssed2023_02007.pdf. Acesso em: 05 ago. 2024.

MENCUCINI, Murilo Silva. **Extrafiscalidade e energia renovável: uma resposta à crise energética e seu uso para o cumprimento de acordos climáticos internacionais**. Trabalho de Conclusão de Curso (Graduação em Direito) – Centro de Ciências Jurídicas, Universidade Federal de Santa Catarina, Florianópolis, 2022. Disponível em: https://repositorio.ufsc.br/bitstream/handle/123456789/233106/TCC%20-EXTRAFISCALIDA%20E%20EN.%20REN.%20MSM.pdf?sequence=1. Acesso em: 10 ago. 2024.

MENZRI, Fatima; DABDOUCHE, Naamane; DEFFAF, Brahim. **Enhancing grid integration of solar energy: a novel approach employing sliding mode control (SMC) and direct power control (DPC) strategies**. Disponível em: https://ijeees.com/wp-content/uploads/2024/08/ID80.pdf. Acesso em: 03 ago. 2024.

MORI, Akihisa; ZHANG, Keyue. Networked sustainable business model innovation and sustainable energy transitions: a case study of incumbent Chinese manufacturers in 2010–2022. **Environmental Innovation and Societal Transitions**, v. 53, p. 100911, 2024.

Disponível em: https://www.sciencedirect.com/science/article/pii/S2210422424001011. Acesso em: 07 ago. 2024.

PAIXÃO, Michel Augusto Santana; MIRANDA, Sílvia Helena Galvão. Um comparativo entre a política de energia renovável no Brasil e na China. **Pesquisa & Debate Revista do Programa de Estudos Pós-Graduados em Economia Política**, v. 29, n. 1 (53), 2018. Disponível em: https://revistas.pucsp.br/rpe/article/download/33934/25963. Acesso em: 02 ago. 2024.

PERIN GASPARIN, Fabiano; BÜHLER, Alexandre José. Panorama atual da geração distribuída no Brasil e o papel da energia solar fotovoltaica no setor. **Avances en Energías Renovables y Medio Ambiente**, v. 22, 2018. Disponível em: https://sedici.unlp.edu.ar/bitstream/handle/10915/108482/Documento_completo.pdf-PDFA.pdf?sequence=1. Acesso em: 07 ago. 2024.

PEYERL, Drielli *et al.* Linkages between the promotion of renewable energy policies and low-carbon transition trends in South America's electricity sector. **Energies**, v. 15, n. 12, p. 4293, 2022. Disponível em: https://www.mdpi.com/1996-1073/15/12/4293/pdf. Acesso em: 06 ago. 2024.

PFLUGMANN, Fridolin Sascha. **Energy and security**: new challenges of the transition to a low-carbon economy. 2020. Tese (Doutorado) – Technische Universität München. Disponível em: https://mediatum.ub.tum.de/doc/1540334/document.pdf. Acesso em: 05 ago. 2024.

PIMENTEL, Paula Emília Oliveira. **Cenários para a transição energética no Brasil 2040**. Tese (Doutorado em Desenvolvimento Sustentável) – Centro de Desenvolvimento Sustentável, Universidade de Brasília, Brasília-DF, 2023. Disponível em: https://repositorio.unb.br/jspui/bitstream/10482/50109/1/2023_PaulaEmiliaOliveiraPimentel_TESE.pdf. Acesso em: 08 ago. 2024.

POURASL, Hamed H.; BARENJI, Reza Vatankhah; KHOJASTEHNEZHAD, Vahid M. Solar energy status in the world: a comprehensive review. **Energy Reports**, v. 10, p. 3474-3493, 2023. Disponível em:

https://www.sciencedirect.com/science/article/pii/S2352484723014579. Acesso em: 07 ago. 2024.

RABELO, Pamela Silva. **Análise da influência da temperatura na eficiência de geração de sistemas de energia solar fotovoltaica com otimizadores de potência.** Monografia (Engenharia de Energias Renováveis) – Centro de Tecnologia, Universidade Federal do Ceará, Fortaleza, 2022. Disponível em: https://repositorio.ufc.br/bitstream/riufc/68971/3/2022_tcc_psrabelo.pdf. Acesso em: 03 ago. 2024.

RATO, Vasco *et al.* Segurança, sustentabilidade e autonomia energética da Europa. **IDN Brief,** 2022. Disponível em: https://comum.rcaap.pt/bitstream/10400.26/42143/1/RATOVasco_SOBRALHugo_COSTAFilipe_RODRIGUESCarlosC_Seguracasustentabilidadeeautonomiaenergeticadaeuropa_IDNBrief_setembro%202022.pdf. Acesso em: 10 ago. 2024.

RINTO, Rinto *et al.* Harnessing the sun: evaluating photovoltaic innovations and smart grid synergies for enhanced renewable energy integration. **GEMOY: Green Energy Management and Optimization Yields**, v. 1, n. 1, p. 23-36, 2024. Disponível em: https://pubcenter.ristek.or.id/index.php/Gemoy/article/download/36/32. Acesso em: 11 ago. 2024.

SAKTHIVADIVEL, D. *et al.* Solar energy technologies: principles and applications. In: Renewable-energy-driven future. **Academic Press**, 2021. p. 3-42. Disponível em: https://www.sciencedirect.com/science/article/pii/B9780128205396000017. Acesso em: 10 ago. 2024.

SILVA, Carlos Rodolfo Vicente da; AMARAL, Breno da Silva. **Viabilidade econômica de um sistema de energia solar fotovoltaica residencial: estudo de caso**. Trabalho de Conclusão de Curso (Bacharelado em Engenharia Civil) – Faculdade de Engenharia Civil, Instituto de Tecnologia, Universidade Federal do Pará, Belém, março, 2023. Disponível em: https://bdm.ufpa.br/bitstream/prefix/6127/1/TCC_ViabilidadeEconomicaSistema.pdf. Acesso em: 02 ago. 2024.

TAVEIRA, Gabriela de Lima. **Energia renovável e tecnologia na América Latina**: desafios para a implementação da ODS 7 - energia limpa e acessível. Trabalho de Conclusão de Curso (Bacharelado em Relações Internacionais) – Instituto de Economia e Relações Internacionais, Universidade Federal de Uberlândia, Uberlândia-MG, 2023. Disponível em: https://repositorio.ufu.br/bitstream/123456789/39469/1/EnergiaRenovavelTecnologia.pdf. Acesso em: 05 ago. 2024.

TEIXEIRA, Layla Leao Lima *et al.* Scenarios and opportunities in the sugar and ethanol industry-challenges and opportunities towards a low carbon economy in Brazil. **Revista de Gestão e Secretariado**, v. 15, n. 1, p. 276-290, 2024. Disponível em: https://ojs.revistagesec.org.br/secretariado/article/download/2996/2056. Acesso em: 10 ago. 2024.

VISHWAKARMA, Neelesh *et al.* **Enhancing solar PV performance**: advanced converters for efficient green energy conversion and grid compatibility. In: E3S Web of Conferences. EDP Sciences, 2024. p. 01137. Disponível em: https://www.e3s-conferences.org/articles/e3sconf/pdf/2024/82/e3sconf_icmpc2024_01137.pdf. Acesso em: 11 ago. 2024.

WAY, Rupert *et al.* Empirically grounded technology forecasts and the energy transition. **Joule**, v. 6, n. 9, p. 2057-2082, 2022. Disponível em: https://www.cell.com/joule/fulltext/S2542-4351(22)00410-X?fbclid=. Acesso em: 10 ago. 2024.

XIAO, Yawei *et al.* Recent advances in carbon nitride-based S-scheme photocatalysts for solar energy conversion. **Materials**, v. 16, n. 10, p. 3745, 2023. Disponível em: https://www.mdpi.com/1996-1944/16/10/3745/pdf. Acesso em: 03 ago. 2024.

ZAYTSEV, Andrey; DMITRIEV, Nikolay; BARYKIN, Sergey. **Resource potential of socio-economic development in the regional sustainability context**: the role of energy security and environment. In: IOP Conference Series: Earth and Environmental Science. IOP Publishing, 2023. p. 012041. Disponível em: https://iopscience.iop.org/article/10.1088/1755-1315/1275/1/012041/pdf. Acesso em: 04 ago. 2024.

ZHENG, Weiye *et al.* **Distributed energy management of multi-entity integrated electricity and heat systems**: a review of architectures, optimization algorithms, and prospects. IEEE

Transactions on Smart Grid, 2023. Disponível em: https://www.researchgate.net/profile/Weiye_Zheng/publication/373623236_Distributed_Energy_Management_of_Multi-Entity_Integrated_Electricity_and_Heat_Systems_A_Review_of_Architectures_Optimization_Algorithms_and_Prospects/links/64fabf4105a98c1b63fc98d1/Distributed-Energy-Management-of-Multi-Entity-Integrated-Electricity-and-Heat-Systems-A-Review-of-Architectures-Optimization-Algorithms-and-Prospects.pdf. Acesso em: 09 ago. 2024.

ZUBLIE, Muhammad Firdaus Mohd; HASANUZZAMAN, Md; RAHIM, Nasrudin Abd. Modeling, energy performance and economic analysis of rooftop solar photovoltaic system for net energy metering scheme in Malaysia. **Energies**, v. 16, n. 2, p. 723, 2023. Disponível em: https://www.mdpi.com/1996-1073/16/2/723/pdf. Acesso em: 05 ago. 2024.

# PATENT CERTIFICATE IN ENGLISH

**SUMMARY**

**Remote Electric Power Generation System**

The mobile energy system (1) of this invention has an industrial nature and consists of the interconnection, via the world wide web, of a virtual photovoltaic plate (2) to be installed in a mobile phone device (3), available for purchase in an application (App)(4), along with the IOS and Android platforms. This virtual photovoltaic panel (2) when installed via App (4), is individually interconnected to a physical photovoltaic panel (5) at a parity of 1 to 1 (1). The interconnection is made through the identity of the code of the physical board with the virtual board downloaded in the application, as well as through an industrial physical device, installed individually on each physical board, interconnected to the application (virtual board) through the world wide web, in order to enable its user, to promote at a distance, the connection and deactivation of solar energy production, through a mechanism made available in its application. Once the actual energy production has begun, the mobile energy system (1) permanently makes available the count of the energy production that has occurred, which will be captured and directly sent to the application (App)( 4) of the holder of the virtual photovoltaic panel (2) corresponding to it.

## DESCRIPTION

### Remote Electric Power Generation System

**Mastery of invention**

The present invention of an industrial nature refers to a system of electric energy production through a virtual photovoltaic panel (2) to be installed in a mobile phone device (3), available for purchase in an application (App)(4), along with the IOS and Android platforms.

World economies are currently focused on researching the increase in the production of energy produced by renewable resources, rethinking their energy matrix by adopting government policies that reward and encourage the creation and development of projects that have innovative and useful ideas for sustainable energy development. It is no longer possible to discredit the global energy crisis, hitherto sustained by its production, through the use of fossil sources.

The world becomes energetic, and the development differential of countries will be directly linked to their ability to transform their energy matrices into clean sources of production, as there is no room for sustainable development, in complete energy dependence combined with exhaustible fossil resources, and with high polluting potential. As a result, recent government strategies are vital for economies, without detracting from their security aspect, resulting from energy dependence.

All new sustainable projects have gained space in the world energy production market, as long as they bring safety mechanisms in low-cost energy generation, with support from renewable sources and satisfactory environmental consequences. More than following the guidelines established in the Kyoto Pact, all nations are currently focused on this new and growing model, tirelessly seeking the affirmation of these new and great definitions, and breaking paradigms.

There is a slowdown in the world economy already installed, and creating cheaper, cleaner and more effective mechanisms for energy production has become a strategy and government policy for several countries. Precisely in this sense, the fact is that in the most developed nations, coal energy production has fallen in recent years by 22%, while there has been an effective increase of 20% in energy production using renewable resources.

It is known that the cost of implementing sustainable factories is already below the implementation of a coal factory. As an example of this democratic transition, Denmark and Germany serve as a model, which propose to invest more in energy produced through the use of hydrogen. Although it still has a high production cost, this method of production and research is the object of development of more accessible techniques.

Specifically in the case of Germany, this country proposes to invest 9 billion euros to encourage the use of hydrogen as a source of green energy production, with 7 billion euros for investment in research, and another 2 billion euros in international partnerships with countries where the so-called "hydrogen can be produced efficiently. It is also home to Morocco and Spain, which are now the two major producers of solar energy in the world.

The system of this invention allows the production of solar energy by users from all over the world, always at a distance, from the acquisition and installation of their virtual board on their mobile phone, individually linked to a physical board installed in the field, anywhere in the world, with the same code number (always in the parity of 1 to 1). The interconnection is made through the identity of the code of the physical board with the virtual board downloaded in the application, as well as through an industrial physical device, installed individually on each physical board, interconnected to the application (virtual board) through the world wide web, in order to enable its user, to promote at a distance, the connection and deactivation of the production of solar energy, through a mechanism made available in its application, a situation that will allow the purchaser to monitor in real time at a distance, its energy produced, through the information stored and provided by the real board, which will be permanently connected to the internet network. Thus, this invention is part of the technical domain of electricity production.

**State of the Art**
According to the IEA (International Energy Agency, 2007), the world energy supply in 2004 was about 11 billion tons of oil equivalent (toe), while the final world energy consumption was about 7.6 billion toe. It is estimated that this

value to grow about 2% per year. This growth rate could be altered if there is a supply crisis, in which high fuel prices would reduce the demand for energy.

The world energy supply (primary energy) is distributed by energy source as follows: oil (34.3%), coal (25.1%), natural gas (20.9%), renewable energy (10.6%), nuclear (6.5%), hydraulic (2.2%) and others (0.4%) (IEA, 2007). The world's final energy consumption is distributed among the following sources: petroleum products (42.3%), electricity (16.2%), natural gas (16.0%), renewable energy (13.7%), coal (8.4%) and others (3.5%). The fuel that has been increasing its participation in the world energy matrix the most is natural gas. The share of coal, which had been declining historically, grew by 1.6% in 2004. Oil, in turn, should remain the main source of world energy until there is a supply restriction, after reaching the peak of world production.

As for electricity, which corresponds to 16.2% of the world's final energy consumption, several primary energy sources contribute to its generation, in the following proportion: 39.8% of coal; 19.6% of natural gas; 16.1% of hydraulic energy; 15.7% from nuclear energy; 6.7% from oil and 2.1% from other energy sources.

**Summary of the Invention**

The present invention of an industrial nature, concerns the mobile energy system ( 1), and consists of the interconnection, via the world internet network, of a virtual photovoltaic panel (2) to be purchased,

downloaded and installed on a mobile phone (3) or computer, available for purchase in an application (App)(4), together with IOS and Android platforms. The virtual board is one of the elements
available in the application, and refers to a virtual image of a normal photovoltaic panel, coupled to the physical plate, through its unique code. In the application, the system also has a control panel and counting of energy production in real time, through access to data permanently available via the internet. This virtual photovoltaic panel (2) when purchased, downloaded and installed, will be individually interconnected to a physical photovoltaic panel (5), in operation and in production, installed in the field for the production of solar energy. The interconnection is made through the identity of the code of the physical board with the virtual board downloaded in the application, as well as through an industrial physical device, installed individually on each physical board, interconnected to the application (virtual board) through the world wide web, in order to enable its user, to promote at a distance, the connection and deactivation of solar energy production, through a mechanism made available in its application (App). The environmental consequences of this policy of a new aspect of growth, supported by clean energy sources, reflect the moment of concern in which the world is looking for solutions for environmental preservation, indispensable for a quality of housing on our planet, combined with economic growth, and its reasons are as follows:

a) Need to immediately reduce the emission of carbon dioxide ($CO_2$) into the atmosphere, and the consensus is scientific;
b) Carbon and carbon dioxide ($CO_2$) are the causes of the so-called "greenhouse effect";
c) Need to reduce the emission of all polluting gases;
d) Sustainable population growth, with an increase in the level of income;
e) Increase in the level of population income without increasing pollution, through change in the energy matrix;
f) Opportunity for new business, and sustainable economic growth with the use of renewable sources that produce ample benefits;
g) Possibility of solar energy production by everyone who does not have physical space to install solar panels in their homes, such as the residents of buildings all over the planet.

h) The great advantage of this invention is that it allows any user to produce energy from anywhere in the world.

**Brief description of the figures**

Figure 1 illustrates the mobile energy system (1) and its functionality, which consists of the interconnection, via the world wide web, of a virtual photovoltaic panel (2) to be installed in a mobile phone device (3), available for purchase in an application (App)( 4) and, when installed, will be individually interconnected to a photovoltaic panel

(5), owned by the company that owns and operates (6) the mobile energy system(1).

Figure 2 shows the mobile phone (3) with the screen displaying the internet page available on the world wide web for access and installation of the mobile energy system (1) through the application

Figure 3 illustrates the mobile phone device (3) with the application registration and access screen (App) (4). Figure 4 illustrates the mobile phone device (3) with the application (App) home screen ( 4), after registration.
Figure 5 shows the mobile phone (3) with the screen showing the devices for the application (App) (4).

Figure 6 illustrates the mobile phone device (3) with the access screen to the power generators in the application (App)(4).

Figure 7 shows the mobile phone (3) with the energy production meters screen in the application (App)(4).

**Preferred achievement description**
As previously mentioned, the mobile energy system (1) of this invention consists of the interconnection, via the world wide web, of a virtual photovoltaic panel (2) to be purchased, downloaded and installed on a mobile phone device (3) or computer, available for purchase in an application (App)(4), along with the IOS and Android platforms.

This virtual photovoltaic panel (2) when acquired, downloaded and installed, will be individually interconnected to a physical photovoltaic panel (5), in operation and in production, installed in the field for the production of solar energy, owned by the company that owns and operates (6) the mobile energy system (1).

In a preferential and more efficient way of realizing this invention, when acquiring and installing the virtual photovoltaic panel (2) accessible in the application (App)(4), energy production will begin within a maximum period of forty-five days, the time necessary to operationalize the installation and individualized interconnection of the virtual photovoltaic panel (2) with a corresponding physical photovoltaic panel (5), implemented in the field, owned by the company that owns and operates (6) the mobile energy system (1).

In a preferential way of carrying out this invention, once the production of real energy in the field has begun, the mobile energy system (1) will make available, at all times, the count of the energy production that has occurred, by permanently sending the production data to the application (App) (4), by means of a worldwide internet network, whose production numbers are permanently captured and sent to the application (App) ( 4), connected to the world wide web, directly to the holder of the virtual photovoltaic panel (2) corresponding to it.

In a preferential way of carrying out this invention, every two months, the company that owns and operates (6) the mobile energy system (1) will provide a final and detailed report of the total individual production in the period, and the financial conversion and monetization of the actual energy production that occurred in the same period, the amount of which will be credited directly to the bank account indicated in the registration in the application (App) (4) by the owner of the virtual photovoltaic panel (2) at the time of the acquisition of the same, or credited through direct rebate in the monthly energy bill, after authorization and agreement to be signed with the existing concessionaires in the market.

**CLAIMS**

1 -The mobile energy system (1) consists of the interconnection, via the world wide web, of a virtual photovoltaic panel (2) to be purchased, downloaded and installed on a mobile phone device (3) or computer. The virtual photovoltaic panel (2) is available for purchase in an application (App) (4), along with IOS and Android platforms. When purchased, downloaded and installed, the virtual photovoltaic panel (2) will be individually interconnected to a physical photovoltaic panel (5), in operation and in production, installed in the field for solar energy production. The physical photovoltaic panel (5) is owned by the company that owns and operates (6) the mobile energy system (1).

2 - The preferential realization of the mobile energy system (1) allows energy production to start within a maximum of forty-five days after the installation and individualized interconnection of the virtual photovoltaic panel (2) with a corresponding physical photovoltaic panel (5), deployed in the field. After the start of real energy production in the field, the mobile energy system (1) will make available at all times the count of the energy production that has occurred, by permanently sending the production data to the application.

3 - The mobile power system can be used in industry to provide remote electrical power to locations where there is no access to the conventional power grid. In addition, the system can be used as an alternative source of electricity to reduce electricity costs and greenhouse gas emissions.

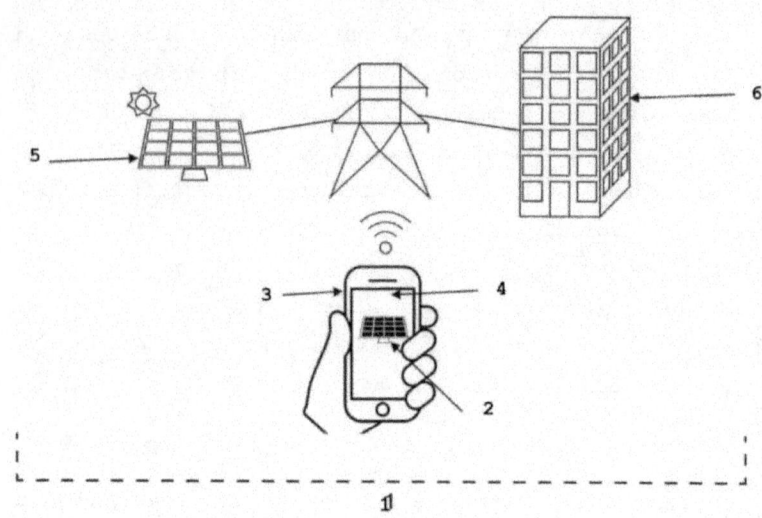

Figure 1

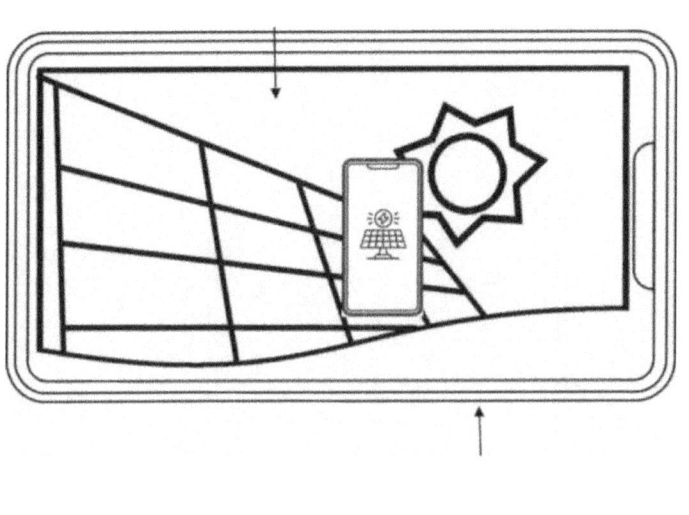

Figure 2

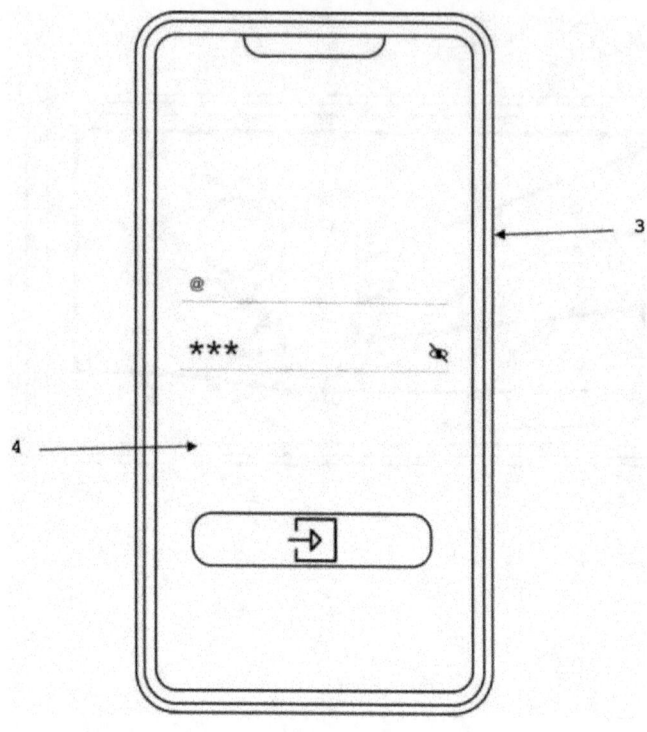

Figure 3

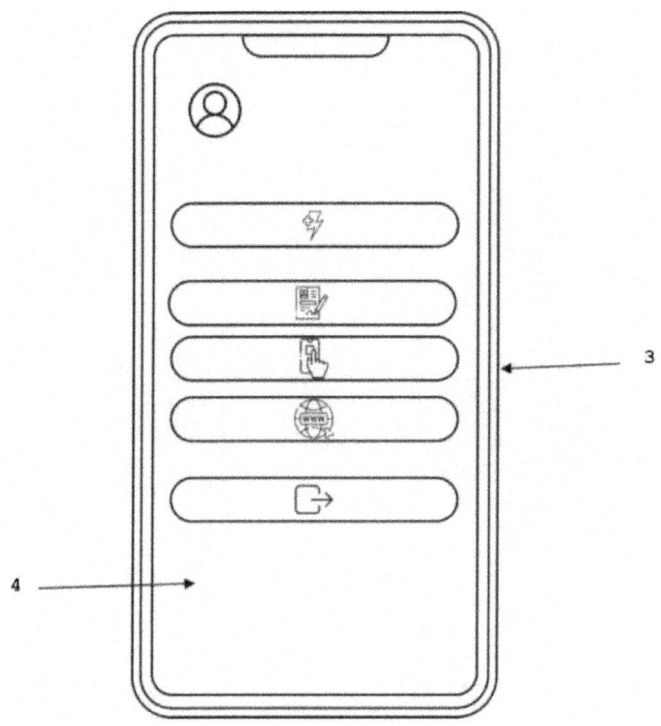

Figure 4

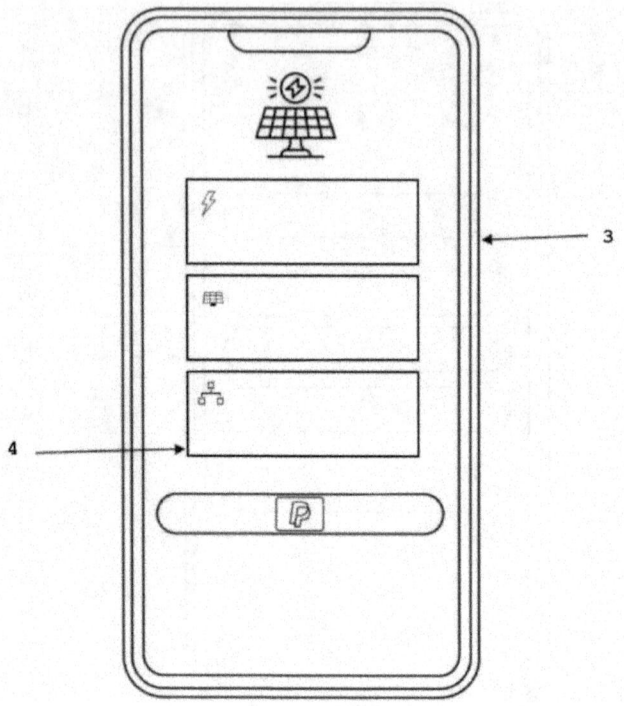

Figure 5

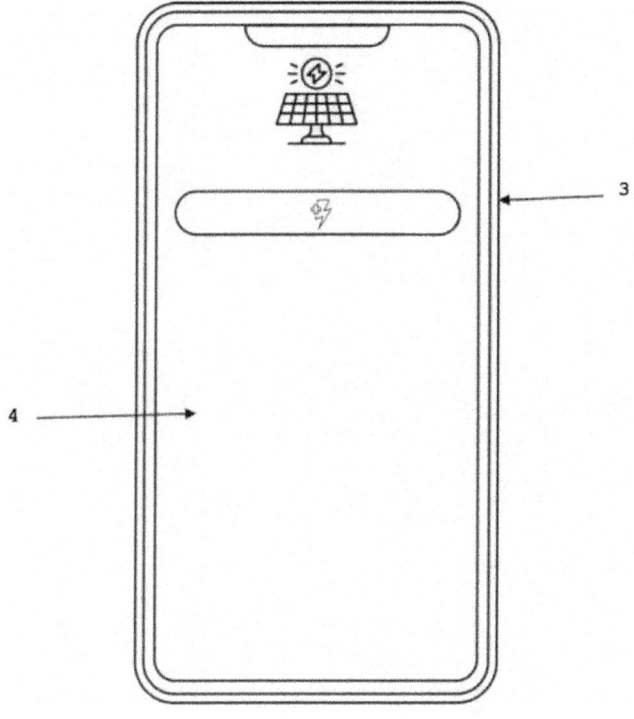

Figure 6

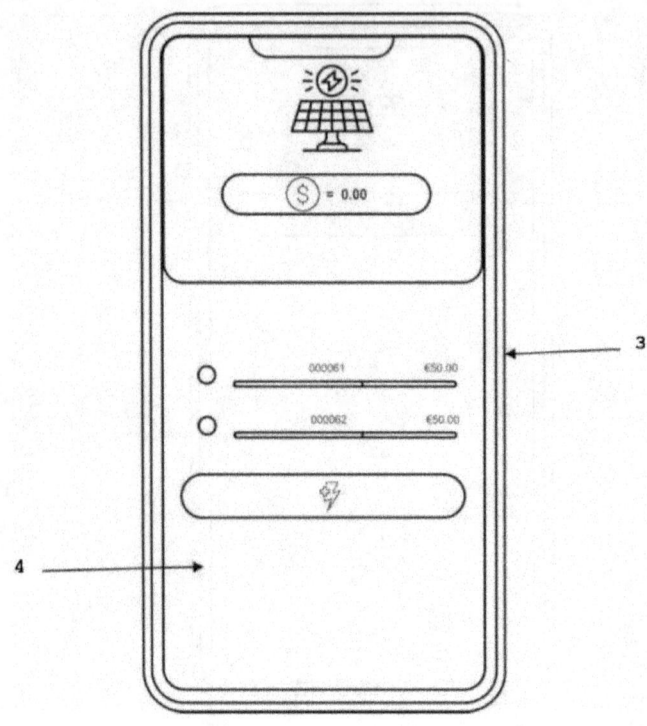

Figure 7

Patent Theme Mobile Photovoltaic Energy

1-Mobile Energy App
Mobile Energy Application is an innovative project for mobile energy production through an application that visualizes the energy production of the photovoltaic panel installed anywhere in the world.
2 - Beneficial of Mobile App ? this application is an investment that can make a profit for companies and individuals, when downloading the application on the Android system the APP automatically appears on the mobile phone screen a photovoltaic energy board showing its daily production of electricity in the property, this energy can be sold in the production company and after the sale the company will deposit the amounts produced in the user's bank account.

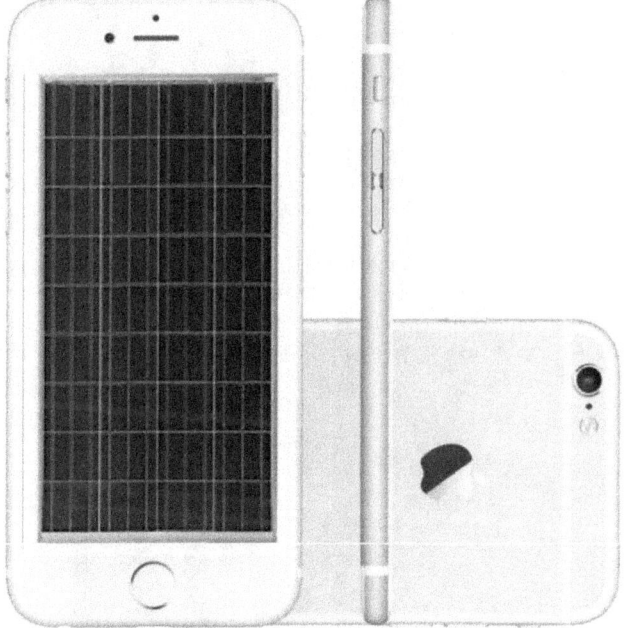

3 - Mobility and benefits ? Anywhere in the world the user will be able to produce their electricity through this application, the great environmental benefit is that the photovoltaic panels will be on farms and power plants where the user does not need to have his photovoltaic plate on the roofs of his house, buildings and apartment, in this case, the user has his plate inside a photovoltaic plant and will not need to maintain his plate since the plates are rights of the owner of the plants

United Plants Photovoltaic Interconnected to Mobile Phone

4 - Usina Unidas Fotovoltaicas, this plant will be an incubator plant of associates owner of the photovoltaic panels and each photovoltaic panel will have an owner who will monitor its energy produced on the mobile phone in the EnergyMovel APP and Android application.

5 - Profits and Partnerships? Each Owner of the EnergyMobile Application will have an interconnection between energy distribution companies with EDP, Iberdrola, Indese, and their production via mobile application can be sold or deducted from the electricity bill or electric car supply, bringing the user a reduction in financial costs and helping the planet reduce $CO_2$ emissions to 0%.

Mobile Interconnection                                   Painel

Mobile Phone Power Generation

## Energy Mobile Phone

Energy Mobile is an innovative project created by Danilo Tadeu Vieira de Sousa, this invention was created to facilitate the production of sustainable electricity without having to set up a factory or put photovoltaic panels on the roof of your house, resident, apartments and company, energy production is 100% via mobile phone behind the application downloading from the Play Store on Android system and App, the production of this energy via Mobile Phone can be sold to Edp, Indesa, Iberdrola or exchanged for consumption in Home or Electric Car, Mobile Energy will have a contract with all local Mobile Energy distribution companies so that the user has the guarantee of financial return on his business and on his Mobile Power Plant.

Mobile Energy Project Mobile Interconnection Telephone with Photovoltaic Plate and Power Plant

Mobile Energy App Android App— Photovoltaic Plate -- Photovoltaic Power Plant

Theme of the Invention Mobile Energy interconnected to Photovoltaic Power Plant, mobile energy production without leaving home ...
Inventor Name Danilo Tadeu Vieira de Sousa
Country Portugal , City Cascais , Address Av Nossa Senhora do Rosário Lote 42 -3D
Cep 2750-181 Bairro do Rosário
B.I 18021056
NIF 230246249
Mobile Phone 00351-936642039

< Danilo Tadeu Vieira de Sousa >

# PATENT CERTIFICATE IN PORTUGUESE

# CERTIFICADO DE PEDIDO PROVISÓRIO DE PATENTE

(11) 116590

Certifica-se que os elementos em anexo estão conforme o original do pedido provisório de patente n.º 116590, apresentado no Instituto Nacional da Propriedade Industrial em 20/07/2020, ao abrigo do artigo 63º do Código da Propriedade Industrial.

(22) Data de pedido: 20/07/2020

(71) Requerente: DANILO TADEU VIEIRA DE SOUSA
AV. NOSSA SENHORA DO ROSÁRIO, 42 - 3 DTO, 2750-181 CASCAIS (PT)

(72) Inventor: DANILO TADEU VIEIRA DE SOUSA (PT)

Estado do processo: PATENTE RECUSADA

(54) Epígrafe: SISTEMA DE GERAÇÃO REMOTA DE ENERGIA ELÉTRICA

(57) Descrição do objeto da invenção: O SISTEMA ENERGIA MÓVEL (1) CONSISTE NA INTERLIGAÇÃO, VIA REDE MUNDIAL DE INTERNET, DE UMA PLACA FOTOVOLTAICA VIRTUAL (2) A SER INSTALADA EM APARELHO DE TELEFONIA MÓVEL (3), DISPONÍVEL PARA AQUISIÇÃO EM APLICATIVO (APP)(4), JUNTO ÀS PLATAFORMAS IOS E ANDROID. ESTA PLACA FOTOVOLTAICA VIRTUAL (2) QUANDO INSTALADA, SERÁ INTERLIGADA INDIVIDUALMENTE A UMA PLACA FOTOVOLTAICA FÍSICA (5), DE PROPRIEDADE DA EMPRESA OPERACIONALIZADORA (6) DO SISTEMA ENERGIA MÓVEL (1). INICIADA A PRODUÇÃO REAL, O SISTEMA ENERGIA MÓVEL (1) DISPONIBILIZARÁ PERMANENTEMENTE A CONTAGEM DA PRODUÇÃO ENERGÉTICA OCORRIDA, QUE SERÁ CAPTADA E DIRETAMENTE ENVIADA AO APLICATIVO (APP)(4) DO TITULAR DA PLACA FOTOVOLTAICA VIRTUAL (2) A ELA CORRESPONDENTE. A CADA PERÍODO BIMENSAL, A EMPRESA OPERACIONALIZADORA (6) DO SISTEMA ENERGIA MÓVEL (1) DISPONIBILIZARÁ UM RELATÓRIO DETALHADO DA PRODUÇÃO TOTAL, E A CONVERSÃO FINANCEIRA DAQUELA PRODUÇÃO ENERGÉTICA, CUJO VALOR SERÁ CREDITADO DIRETAMENTE EM CONTA BANCÁRIA INDICADA NO CADASTRO PELO TITULAR DA PLACA FOTOVOLTAICA VIRTUAL (2).

Instituto Nacional da Propriedade Industrial,

18/10/2024

Pela Chefe de Departamento,

Inês Cristóvão da Silva

A Responsável,

Teresa Paula Pinto

Instituto Nacional da Propriedade e Industrial (INPI)

Assinado de forma digital por Instituto Nacional da Propriedade Industrial (INPI)
Dados: 2024.10.21 11:02:54 +01'00'

M0681.03

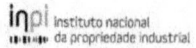
**Instituto nacional da propriedade industrial**

Campo das Cebolas - 1149-035 Lisboa - Portugal
Tel: +351 218818100 / Linha Azul: 808 200689 / Fax: +351 218875308 / Fax: +351 218860066 / E-mail: atm@inpi.pt / www.inpi.pt

| Nº | CÓDIGO | DATA E HORA DE RECEÇÃO | MODALIDADE | PROCESSO RELACIONADO |
|---|---|---|---|---|
| 20211000027691 | 0121 | 2021/07/16-07:43:39 | PAT | 116590 X |

PAGAMENTO CONFIRMADO

## OUTROS ATOS - PATENTES, MODELOS DE UTILIDADE OU TOPOGRAFIA DE PRODUTOS SEMICONDUTORES

### 1 REQUERENTE

**Código**
**Nome** DANILO TADEU VIEIRA DE SOUSA
**Endereço** AVENIDA NOSSA SENHORA DO ROSÁRIO, 42 - 3 DIREITO
**Localidade** CASCAIS
**Telefone**      **Telemóvel** 936642039
**E-mail** PROF.ENG.DR.DANILOSOUSA@GMAIL.COM
**Atividade (CAE)** 35113
**NIF** 230246249

**Nacionalidade** PORTUGUESA

**Código Postal** 2750-181
**Fax**

**Tipo de Representação** Advogado, solicitador ou outra pessoa com procuração
**Nome** BRAZ LABANCA NETO
**Endereço** PRACETA QUINTA DONA MARIA, 3 R/C FTE.
**Localidade** SEIXAL
**Telefone**      **Telemóvel** 913748223
**E-mail** BRAZLABANCA@GMAIL.COM

**Código**

**Código Postal** 2840-497
**Fax**

### 2 ACTO REQUERIDO

### 3 DOCUMENTOS ANEXOS

FOTOCÓPIA DE BI (PDF B I DANILO BILHETE DE IDENTIDADE.pdf)
OUTROS (ENERGIA MÓVEL Memorial descritivo PEDIDO DEFINITIVO INPI.pdf)
OUTROS (PROCURACAO DANILO BRAZ.pdf)
FOTOCÓPIA DE BI (PDF BRAZ CARTEIRA PROFISSIONAL.pdf)

### 4 OBSERVAÇÕES

CUMPRIMENTO A DMP/DGD/01/2021/1927399 - REFERENTE PATENTE DE INVENÇÃO NACIONAL N. 116590 - DE 2021/01/27APRESENTAÇÃO DE PEDIDO DE CONVERSÃO DE PEDIDO PROVISÓRIO EM DEFINITIVO DENTRO DO PRAZO LEGALANEXO - DOCUMENTO CONTENDO REIVINDICAÇÕES - DESCRIÇÃO DO OBJECTO DA INVENÇÃO - DESENHOS NECESSÁRIOS - RESUMO DA INVENÇÃOPRAZO FINAL PARA APRESENTAÇÃO DO PEDIDO DE CONVERSÃO: 20/07/2021

O Requerente e o INPI acordam em submeter a Tribunal Arbitral eventuais litígios emergentes do presente ato, nos termos e condições especificados em Anexo. Esta cláusula vincula as partes que a subscrevem, apenas podendo ser revogada, por comum acordo, até à pronúncia da decisão arbitral.

Autorizo que os meus dados sejam utilizados para efeitos de inquérito sobre a qualidade dos serviços on-line do INPI.

Autorizo que os meus dados sejam facultados ao ARBITRARE Centro de Arbitragem para a Propriedade Industrial, Nomes de Domínio, Firmas e Denominações, a fim de que este centro me possa esclarecer e informar sobre os respetivos serviços de mediação e arbitragem.

## 5 TAXAS

| Taxa | Importância |
|---|---|
| CONVERSÃO DE PED. PROV. DE PATENTE EM DEFINITIVO | 75,42 € |
| Total: | 75,42 € |
| Por Extenso: | SETENTA E CINCO EUROS E QUARENTA E DOIS CÊNTIMOS |

## 6 PAGAMENTO

| | |
|---|---|
| Tipo de Pagamento | Multibanco/Homebanking |
| Entidade | 10587 |
| Referência | 070 936 274 |
| Montante | 75,42 € |
| Data Limite de Pagamento | 19-07-2021 |

Poderá efetuar o pagamento em qualquer Caixa Multibanco (opção pagamento de serviços/compras) ou serviço de Homebanking (opção Pagamento de Compras).

Se, ao efetuar o pagamento, for necessária a seleção de "pagamentos de compra" e o respetivo pagamento não for possível, deverá contactar a sua entidade bancária no sentido de verificar se o cartão bancário que está a utilizar tem essa função ativa.

Nos termos da alínea a) do n.º 1 do artigo 24.º do Código da Propriedade Industrial, fica por este meio notificado para proceder ao pagamento do ato solicitado no prazo de três dias. Findo este prazo, e na ausência de pagamento, o ato solicitado poderá ser alvo de recusa/indeferimento.

## 7 ASSINATURA DO REQUERENTE OU MANDATÁRIO/REPRESENTANTE LEGAL

**Assinatura/Nome** BRAZ LABANCA NETO
**Nº B.I.** YB0410708        **Data** 2021/07/16

**Atenção:** Os dados relativos ao nome e morada serão publicados no Boletim da Propriedade Industrial, de acordo com o previsto no Código da Propriedade Industrial, aprovado pelo Decreto-Lei n.º 36/2003, de 5 de Março, ficando também incluídos nas bases de dados de marcas e patentes disponibilizadas neste portal.
Se desejar que a morada não seja conhecida pode optar por indicar um Apartado Postal.
Caso o requeira, poderá também aceder e retificar os seus dados. Para mais informações consulte a política de privacidade deste portal.

**inpi** instituto nacional
da propriedade industrial

Campo das Cebolas - 1149-035 Lisboa - Portugal
Tel: +351 218818100 / Linha Azul: 808 200689 / Fax: +351 218875308 / Fax: +351 218860066 / E-mail: atm@inpi.pt / www.inpi.pt

| N° | CÓDIGO | DATA E HORA DE RECEÇÃO | MODALIDADE | PROCESSO RELACIONADO |
|---|---|---|---|---|
| 20201000036398 | 0198 | 2020/07/20-18:36:30 | PAT | 116590 X |

PAGAMENTO CONFIRMADO

## PEDIDO DE PATENTE, MODELO DE UTILIDADE OU DE TOPOGRAFIA DE PRODUTOS SEMICONDUTORES

### 1  REQUERENTE

**Código**  
**Nome** DANILO TADEU VIEIRA DE SOUSA  
**Nacionalidade** PORTUGUESA  
**Endereço** AVENIDA NOSSA SENHORA DO ROSÁRIO, 42 - 3 DIREITO  
**Localidade** CASCAIS  
**Código Postal** 2750-181  
**Telefone** 936642039  **Telemóvel** 936642039  **Fax**  
**E-mail** PROF.ENG.DR.DANILOSOUSA@GMAIL.COM  
**Atividade (CAE)**  
**NIF** 230246249  

**Tipo de Representação** Advogado, solicitador ou outra pessoa com procuração  
**Nome** BRAZ LABANCA NETO  **Código**  
**Endereço** PRACETA QUINTA DONA MARIA, 3 R/C FTE.  
**Localidade** SEIXAL  
**Código Postal** 2840-497  
**Telefone** 913748223  **Telemóvel** 913748223  **Fax**  
**E-mail** brazlabanca@gmail.com  

### 2  MODALIDADE / TIPO DE PEDIDO

Modalidade: PEDIDO PROVISÓRIO DE PATENTE  
Realização de pesquisa pelo INPI: SIM  

### 3  EPÍGRAFE OU TÍTULO

ENERGIA MÓVEL PROJECTO DE PRODUÇÃO DE ENERGIA ELÉCTRICA SOLAR ATRAVÉS DO TELEMÓVEL APLICATIVO APP ANDROID, IOS, TABLETES, NOTEBOOKS, COMPUTADORES E SMART TV

### 4  RESUMO

### 5  FIGURAS

### 6  INVENTORES

**Nacionalidade** PORTUGUESA  
**Nome** DANILO TADEU VIEIRA DE SOUSA  
**Endereço** AVENIDA NOSSA SENHORA DO ROSÁRIO, 42 - 3 DIREITO  
**Localidade** CASCAIS  
**Código Postal** 2750-181  
**Telefone** 936642039  **Telemóvel** 936642039  
**E-mail** PROF.ENG.DR.DANILOSOUSA@GMAIL.COM  
**NIF** 230246249

| 7 | REIVINDICAÇÃO DE PRIORIDADE |
|---|---|

| 8 | DOCUMENTOS ANEXOS |
|---|---|

OUTROS (ARQUIVO PEDIDO PATENTE.pdf)
DOCUMENTO DO PEDIDO PROVISÓRIO DE PATENTE (ARQUIVO PEDIDO PATENTE.pdf)

| 9 | OBSERVAÇÕES |
|---|---|

Invenção tecnológica de autoria e propriedade exclusiva do Dr. Danilo Tadeu Vieira de Sousa de nome Energia Móvel. Desenvolvimento de aplicativo (software) baixado em aparelhos de telefonia móvel, notebooks e tablets, correspondente com uma placa fotovoltaica física em funcionamento na usina. Assim, a energia solar é produzida por todos que não dispõem de espaço físico para um sistema tradicional em suas residências. O aplicativo mobile e a placa fotovoltaica são interligados através da integração de seus softwares, que possibilita a transmissão de dados e informações originadas da usina por sistema de internet. A placa física capta radiação solar e a transforma em energia elétrica renovável, e o usuário tem acesso contínuo da produção de energia diretamente na sua placa virtual, em tempo real, através do aplicativo. No contador virtual instalado, os usuários recebem relatórios periódicos, permitindo a conferência da quantidade de energia produzida, e sua monetização, concedendo-lhe lucro na operação do sistema.

O Requerente e o INPI acordam em submeter a Tribunal Arbitral eventuais litígios emergentes do presente ato, nos termos e condições especificados em Anexo. Esta cláusula vincula as partes que a subscrevem, apenas podendo ser revogada, por comum acordo, até à pronúncia da decisão arbitral.

Autorizo que os meus dados sejam utilizados para efeitos de inquérito sobre a qualidade dos serviços on-line do INPI.

Autorizo que os meus dados sejam facultados ao ARBITRARE Centro de Arbitragem para a Propriedade Industrial, Nomes de Domínio, Firmas e Denominações, a fim de que este centro me possa esclarecer e informar sobre os respetivos serviços de mediação e arbitragem.

| 10 | TAXAS |
|---|---|

| Taxa | Importância |
|---|---|
| PEDIDO PROVISÓRIO DE PATENTE | 10,79 € |
| PESQUISA EM PEDIDO PROVISÓRIO DE PATENTE | 53,93 € |
| Total: | 64,72 € |
| Por Extenso: | SESSENTA E QUATRO EUROS E SETENTA E DOIS CÊNTIMOS |

| 11 | PAGAMENTO |
|---|---|

| Tipo de Pagamento | Multibanco/Homebanking |
|---|---|
| Entidade | 10587 |
| Referência | 064 092 660 |
| Montante | 64,72 € |
| Data Limite de Pagamento | 23-07-2020 |

Poderá efetuar o pagamento em qualquer Caixa Multibanco (opção pagamento de serviços/compras) ou serviço de Homebanking (opção Pagamento de Compras).

Se, ao efetuar o pagamento, for necessária a seleção de "pagamentos de compra" e o respetivo pagamento não for possível, deverá contactar a sua entidade bancária no sentido de verificar se o cartão bancário que está a utilizar tem essa função ativa.

Nos termos da alinea a) do n.º 1 do artigo 24.º do Código da Propriedade Industrial, fica por este meio notificado para proceder ao pagamento do ato solicitado no prazo de três dias. Findo este prazo, e na ausência de pagamento, o ato solicitado poderá ser alvo de recusa/indeferimento.

| 12 | ASSINATURA DO REQUERENTE OU MANDATÁRIO/REPRESENTANTE LEGAL |
|---|---|

Assinatura/Nome DANILO TADEU VIEIRA DE SOUSA
Nº B.I. 18021056                                                      Data 2020/07/20

Atenção: Os dados relativos ao nome e morada serão publicados no Boletim da Propriedade Industrial, de acordo com o previsto no Código da Propriedade Industrial, aprovado pelo Decreto-Lei n.º 36/2003, de 5 de Março, ficando também incluídos nas bases de dados de marcas e patentes disponibilizadas neste portal.
Se desejar que a morada não seja conhecida pode optar por indicar um Apartado Postal.
Caso o requeira, poderá também aceder e retificar os seus dados. Para mais informações consulte a política de privacidade deste portal.

## ABOUT THE AUTHOR

Man in suit and tie with a book in his hand
Automatic description
Danilo dedicated himself to his studies in the best schools and universities in Brazil and Europe. He has completed courses at several respected institutions, including:
SENAI Polytechnic School: General Mechanic
Francisco Ferreira Lopes Technical School: Accounting Sciences
Universidade Nova de Lisboa: Master's Degree in Spatial Planning, Post-graduation in Environmental Education
Universidade Grande Dourado, Brazil: Graduated in Real Estate Territorial Management, Technologist in Environmental Impact Engineering
Montes Claros University (RA272845): Post-graduation in Environmental Engineering, Technician in Biosphere and Biodiversity Analysis
Monte Carlos University: Degree in Biological Sciences
Curricular Extension in Fine Arts - Sculpture of Cities
MERAK University, Vigo, Spain: Master and Captain of Navigation
Danilo brings a wealth of knowledge and experience that is reflected in his work, uniting his passion for art, science, and innovation in every project he undertakes.

www.ingramcontent.com/pod-product-compliance
Lightning Source LLC
Chambersburg PA
CBHW070159230526
45471CB00002B/726